A CONFESSION

I realize that in this book, I have been redundant and repetitious.
I am eighty years old and remember more of the past than what I did
or said five minutes ago.
Forgive me, I'm sorry about that, overlook this failing, plunge ahead and enjoy.
Pictures of one of my many sculptures on the cover and others inside.
Trust, but verify.
Definition of Propinquity
Nearness in time or place
Nearness of Relationship: Kinship
The key word resulting in a satisfactory marriage.
Both parties must respect one another. It's called love.
If we didn't love somebody, nobody would be here.

The Author,
Norman A. Richards

TABLE OF CONTENTS

The Start Of Your Journey

Since most of all males are aware that it is an almost impossible task to discover what females gossip about, I endeavor to point out a few topics that they may discuss.

Not being able to ever know for sure, I submit some naive delving into possible scenarios.

I also reveal many of my personal experiences, observations and commonly used terminology of sayings, dirty words and body parts, as well as human body linkages.

Conservative beliefs and warnings of the impending possible catastrophe should the socialists, left wing radicals and the danger if the democrats should gain the white house and complete control of this country, not a pretty picture!

If you can be truthful with yourself, I am sure that you must agree that you have been there – done this – done that.

Maybe a smile and a nod of agreement in here, too. Laughing out loud is allowed. Shake a leg, me hearties.

Sigmund Freud admitted that he could never figure out what women want!? Answer, who can?

Too many of us live in silent desperation trying and trying to find and to see the light at the end of the tunnel.

Forward

It is reported that women speak at least 20,000 words a day. Men only about 7,000 words, if they can get'em in.

"But the liberal deviseth liberal things; and by liberal things shall he stand."
ISAIAH 32:8

"When that great score keeper in the sky comes to judge you, makes no difference whether you won or lost, but how you played the games." Grantland Rice, Sports Writer

A friend says to his pal, "I think that my wife is frigid." Never answer, "Oh, no she isn't!"

I get sex almost every day. Almost on Monday, almost on Tuesday and almost on and on.

Women don't want to hear what you think. Women want to hear what they think – in a deeper voice.
Bill Cosby

What I need is to find a woman who loves me for my money but doesn't understand math.
Mike Birbiglia

An optimist is one who believes marriage is a gamble.
Laurence J. Peter

A man is incomplete until he is married. After that, he is finished.
Zsa Zsa Gabor

Most women set out to change a man and when they have changed him, they do not like him.
Marlene Dietrich

Most men who rail against women are railing at one woman only.
Remy De Gourmont

The highest level of sexual excitement is in a monogamous relationship.
Warren Beatty

There is no substitute for the comfort supplied by the utterly taken-for–granted relationship.
Iris Murdoch

Shared joy is double joy, and shared sorrow is half sorrow.
Swedish Proverb

As the Spanish say, there are no roses without thorns.
Anon

In the morning I have quarterheimers, at noon, halfheimers, at cocktail hour, I have full blown Alzheimers.
Norm

If you would not step into the harlot's house, do not go by the harlot's door.
Socrates

Conscience is what hurts when everything feels so good.

"Daddy, what is heredity?" "Heredity, my boy, is what a man believes in until his son begins to act like a fool."

"How'd you get along with your wife in that fight the other night?" "Awe, she came crawling to me on her knees." "Yeah? What's she say?" "Come out from under the bed, you coward."

One man read so much about the bad effects of drinking that he decided to give up reading.

"Do you know that they don't hang men with wooden legs in China?" "Zat so?" "Why?" "They use rope."

As Onslo says on the PBS TV show keeping up appearances, "OH!, NICE!"

PLAY BALL! BALL SOMEONE! Don't ask me what that means as I will only deny knowing.

GREETING EUPHEMISMS

What's your favorite name or method of greeting or getting the attention of the little woman?

Hi, Babe
Hi, My Darling
Hi, Sweetie
Hi, Sugarplum
Sweetie Pie
Hi, Doll
Honey Bunch
Hi, My Squeeze
Honey Bug or Bun
Hi, Angel
Hey, Lover
Hi, Mom
Love of My Life
Hi, Pussycat
Hi, Gorgeous
You're the Greatest
Hi, Number One
Love You, Babe

Question, "Where's your girlfriend, love of your life?" Answer, "I forgot where I laid her."

Eve's famous question – "Want an apple, Honey?"

PROLOGUE:
WHAT DO WOMEN GOSSIP ABOUT?

Women, who are primarily controlled by the left side of their brains, are adept in the use of words.

They can become fixated with one thought and will refuse all other explanations and answers.

Men hear their particular point that they expound and since conversation is so slow, the men can think of many diverse ways to solve the problem posed. While listening or feigning to do so, conclude that there is not just one answer.

Of course, obviously many alternative solutions, interpretations of usage and feel compelled to interrupt and present their side of what is right and why she may be wrong and perhaps way off base in reasoning.

She may have only one thought at a time trapped by the left side of her brain – Dictionary meaning of words. She will resist any attempt to clarify her reasoning.

Should a man, somehow succeed in stopping her flow and get to outline what he considers proper, it is to no avail. No matter how good he creates logical examples, citing facts, figures and recalls other situations, it is a losing cause.

Let's face it, she has heard nothing to change her mind and continues on with her viewpoint. No matter how long you evade her, upon reconfronting you again, she will pick right up – continue her attack. Give up, knowing that you can't win for losing.

She is convinced that she is right and maddenly go right ahead with her ingrained belief.

It appears that from childhood the female sex is astute with verbalization. The human brain is bicameral and has a left hemispherical side and a right side.

The reliance on the left brain in thoughts and reasoning alone can be calculating and devious.

The right brain is more attuned to the visual and is more imaginary, seeing patterns and how things go together to create that which side has its own particular abilities and methods of perceiving reality.

Our right brain can be tricked by the left brain into false ideals. Herein lies the big problem.

Since the right brain thinks in past pictures stored therein and not in words, it is known that under hypnosis the right side can recall vivid details of some past occurrences and situations.

The ability to rapidly use both left and right sides to see an answer and conclusion is paramount. Too much reliance on one side primarily can allow one to come up with the wrong evaluation.

The right side can solve complex problems which elude the use of the left brain solely. The right brain is great at recognizing shapes and how they relate to one another. It has hidden abilities such as music and sports skills. Of course, some women do too.

Thus absorbing these givens, it is obvious to me that one who uses mostly the left brain in their conversations as logical, may be unreasonably, perhaps wrong in their feelings that they are always undoubtedly correct in their thinking.

Therein lies the problem in any debate or confrontation.

HO, HO, HO,
It's nice to be young
HO, HO, HO,
I feel great
Do this ditty and you'll see how much better you will be.
Shout, I feel great
And it's nice to be young
Absolutely needs to be sung
You will feel great
And so will your mate
So, sing Ho, Ho, Ho
It's nice to be young
Let's face it, no matter your age
You'll feel great at being a sage
Here's my comment, not just for the moment
I feel great and Ho, Ho, Ho it's nice to be young
Shout it out loud
You'll feel proud.
Ho, Ho, Ho!

By NAR

FEELING LOW AND DEPRESSED?

Whenever you're down, depressed and feel blue, stop whatever you are doing and shout, I mean it, Shout, "I feel great!" Do it again, I dare you to not feel better.

"I feel great." Troubles are gone!

I am confident that all of my readers, if they are honest with themselves will deep down admit that they have been there, done that and that we all are sinners. You know that however hard that it is to admit, you have heard the terms used and are aware of the actions, scenarios depicted in this book. Be honest, admit it. Confession is good for the soul.

I am sure that my impressions, stories and ideas may not have been all factually correct. Like my artistic endeavors, when asked why I did so and so, I have no answer. They are never completed to my satisfaction and often added to or altered.

My answer has to be that my hand and my mind are guided by some higher power. The good things created are God influenced and the shady, bad things must be the work of the Devil who made me do it!

"Ho, Ho, Ho, IT'S NICE TO BE YOUNG!
Ho, Ho, Ho, I FEEL GREAT!"

Laugh and the world laughs with you. You'll feel great if you sing. Smile a lot, too. It couldn't hoit! The secret to a longer, satisfying life in there somewhere.

The So-called Gossiping Weaker Sex?

I've watched, studied, ogled the ladies abroad many times as well as here and every where else. These mysterious women have been an enigma to me since childhood. What are they doing and talking about? Does anyone really know?

At a young age, I watched little girls, huddle together, giggle and keep their eyes trained on we boys. I always wondered what they were looking at, thinking about and most of all what is so important for them to talk about seemingly for an eternity?

To this day, I am amazed at what two women find to talk about for hours on end?

Have you ever witnessed the meeting of two ladies who meet for the first time and how they converse forever?

More often than not, daughters gravitate to their fathers. This is early training for them to be close to, observe and to learn to charm the pants off of men. They quickly learn the secrets of gaining approval and attention from men. The hapless man is drawn into their web of desire, influence and control.

Later in age, I saw first hand what a woman goes through during her menstrual period. I was daydreaming in high school study hall, when a pretty girl seated nearby, started crying out loud and when I looked at her, I saw blood running off of her seat onto the floor. Thank goodness there was a lady proctor in charge of the room and she came quickly to escort the girl out to calm her down and tell her that it is normal and not to be ashamed of what had happened to her.

That was my first, first-hand experience seeing what women have to endure to expunge their bodies and to begin to prepare for the next monthly onslaught to be prepared to have her eggs ready to be possibly implanted with the male sperm and thus the marvel of creating a baby.

I had early on in life been exposed to the distinguishing, disgusting odor and smell of a disposed Kotex-type napkin. Could this subject be one of the topics of which women discuss? We men are never privy to such information.

Okay, here's a short idea of what goes on in a woman, as I understand it. The male sperm injected into the lady swims up the fallopian tubes. It can live for up to six days before the release of her egg. Also up to twenty four hours afterwards.

The woman's pelvic bones shelter the fallopian tubes, the ovary, the uterus, the cervix, on down to the bladder, the vagina, the urethra, the clitoris and the vulva. The hard and sharp pelvic bones can make for a painful and unpleasant ride on the gal's body.

Breaking a girl's maiden head (Hymen we call her cherry) is most looked forward to and desirous by men, with all of these different parts of her nomenclature, do you think any gossiping goes on about their functions?

Poor lonely woman

We male-like creatures are paranoid when seeing a group of ladies looking in our direction whispering and giggling. It is very disarming and disconcerting with no answer ever known of what had just transpired.

Like little kids, we wonder what have I done wrong now? We learn early on to be suspicious of everything that girls and women do. Thus, we never exactly know what motivates the opposite sex.

Perhaps the primary mastery and reliance on the left side of her brain by females is the answer as to why men will never understand them. They seemingly cannot accept that their one sided limited understanding of a perplexing problem has more plausible answers to the dilemma posed and it is seemingly impossible for them to grasp, understand, comprehend and even consider anything else at that point in time. Sorry repetition coming.

Human beings have a bicameral brain, the right side of the brain sees, stores, experiences thousands of sights and sounds daily and processes them.

It is the left side of one's brain which is logical, recognizes words and their meanings. The right side of the brain is used more by men. It stores all that we have seen and known. We can cull through these archives in a micro second and use our left side of our brain to check the truth and logic of what is right and best to be done.

Of course, there are many women who properly make use of the both sides of their brains and we men have to sheepishly admit that maybe they are right.

This not being a scholarly treatise on these mysterious human attributes, it is obvious to the reader that expando has pontificated a whole bunch here.

Just a form of male gossiping by me and to be absorbed or not by you and as Walter Cronkite says, "That's the way it is."

Again, as Sigmund Freud admitted, he never could discover what women want?

Women, they will defend their analysis and side in a controversy to the bitter end.

They will become increasingly irate the longer one tries to point out where they are wrong and are in error in their position and thinking. In the long run after a serious encounter with much give and take, the man may come to see that the conviction of her belief and argument may have some truth to it and merit to the possible consequences.

It is tough though for a man to admit it. From this hypothetical confrontation of questionable importance, I have to admit that I am not an authority on any subject and don't claim to be such.

Better to back off, swallow your pride and just walk away and allow her to think that she is right and has won her point.

Don't sweat the small stuff. Everything is small stuff.

One should not go around looking for trouble and trying to start a fight.

Think Ahead! There's always a rub.

What does a man think about while he is humping? Not much, mostly how can I stop from coming too fast. All's right with the world and nothing else matters. Right?

MOTOR MOUTHS

You have all heard and used this expression to refer to talkative individuals. These people will monopolize any and all situations and babble on and on.

They have a tendency to by-pass the topic at hand and start off in an entirely different direction with their comments.

Almost, look at me-listen to me-I know what is right and has to be said, boring though it may be.

They may get quite exercised, boisterous and animated with their unwanted pap.

This sort of a person reminds me of a nameless, well known politician who is always seeking an opportunity to be seen on TV and to be heard.

Wherever members of the press are gathered interviewing some personage, this clown comes a running, interrupts the routine questioning and takes over with his own ideas and beliefs and the original topic on previously, is long gone and the amazing, boring rant goes on. This display of brash, not asked for, lengthy crap goes on by him at every opportunity and is a disgrace and disservice to all men folk.

Motor mouths of both gender are to be avoided at all costs if possible - oh, my aching ears!

SPECULATION ON MEN'S BEHAVIOR

It must have to do with the right side of the brain
Thinking and childhood experiences-practice

Young boys, from an early age, explore what happens when some object held in their hand and then thrown reacts. They learn with practice to become quite accurate with their throws and get an idea of what is involved solving the trajectory required. Grasping, tossing in one's hand and ready to go.

These activities are all computed automatically by the world's greatest computer - their brain. From early on, any object to be thrown, is a fun thing to do, I soon became quite efficient and accurate throwing different sized stones at a specific target selected in my mind in advance.

One day, a museum curator visiting us, was in the backyard of our home. I was gathering huge, green covered walnuts. Seeing me, he said that he would bet that I could throw one at a utility pole some 40 feet away and hit it. Completely confident, I wound up like a baseball pitcher and hurled a perfectly impacted strike on the pole. I was proud, but didn't consider the fete to be anything special for me to do. Dead center.

Boys-men learn automatically how to judge distances, widths and depths. Of course we learn how to alter the trajectory according to the situation involved and wind trajectory, second nature to us.

Women seem to have other things on their minds and are not anywhere adept at such male-type doings. I quite frankly, believe that a women automobile driver is not aware of the rear of the car and only what is up front and to the right and left of her shoulders. There's a whole lot of car left back there.

Eyeballing objects, men mentally estimate weights, sizes and distances without much thinking or guessing about it.

Not many women can visualize and do many mechanical things. Men are more adept at fixing things, we do it more.

MORE MUSINGS ON MALE WORRIES

Are these ladies private moments with their friends really much ado about nothing? I'm sure that the girl friends have a tendency to let slip a personal happening to them, their husband's actions surely come into play and once one confesses, the flood gates reopen to reveal each and everyone's grisly details. A man can never rest assured that what goes on in a hen party gathering, what is said, what is discussed and how much has been revealed.

It all comes down to how much you can trust your lady and believe what she tells you.

The man who doesn't give a bloody damn one way nor another is to be complemented or considered a stupid fool. Always damned if you do and damned if you don't.

Women will be women and God love them, but they retain their secrets and can hold stuff against you and cut off their sexual favors.

They relish their power that they hold over their hapless mates. They generally outlive the men and wind up controlling most of the money in the world.

Of course, we should pity the male slobs who go through life continuing to wonder, what do women gossip about? Men can contract a neurosis and wind up trusting nobody.

We come into this world alone and exit it alone.

Unfortunately, in many cases, once the man has been captured in marriage, it soon becomes the end of the comely, lovely looking lady - slobsville here she comes.

Once the hunt is over and in total command of her little domain, you can rest assured that change is in the offing. Her personal attention to her daily beauty care will soon go to pot and become less important to her.

They have won their prey and no need to be obsessed with all of the pre-marriage attention to looking nice, always not caring about her appearance anymore.

One day, it will come to your attention that her hips seem to be growing wider. No worry, softer landing pad, this is especially true when rolls of fat come on her belly, she is not worried, to hell with it, I've got my man.

A woman's physical beauty is transitory and disappears much sooner than her male counterpart, unfortunately. Men are told that they have aged more slowly and look very distinguished. Not always as sometimes the two begin to look like each other, fat and all.

I have made women mad at me for saying to her that she looks divine as she advances, but has she seen herself retreating?

Me and my big mouth. Lost a bunch that way. The truth hurts and sometimes has to be said.

I have noticed that women just adore and envy, say a male athlete who has a tiny-firm ass. This must be one of the main worries that women have about aging and mid-life spread. They are fascinated by asses.

I get a kick - try it yourself - pay attention as any woman walks away from you and guess how long it takes her to turn her head back towards you to see if you are watching her leave. She attempts to get eye contact with you to divert your eyes from her undulating hips. Or is it her satisfaction to have gotten your attention?

ON THE OTHER HAND SHE HAD WARTS

What we have here is an answer. When no other cogent thoughts to offer is on the other hand she has warts.

We are dealing with an extremely smart, crafty, dangerous siren on the make. Having caught you watching her retreat, she is very happy to have succeeded.

Of course, it is true that an approaching vixen attracts the male first by his savoring her total body shape men look at and want those boobs to be his alone. He checks her hair, her face, nose size and lip size. A full lower lip is desirous. Many enlarged on purpose with collagen injections. White pearly glistening straight teeth a must. The size of her belly and swaying hips another quick checkout. If you are lucky and she is one of a dead breed of temptresses who wears a short dress and not long pants, long exciting legs-gams a plus.

Early on in a woman's search for the ideal mate, she will accept an invitation to go to any affair with any slug who asks her to go. Being seen there is upper most to the thing that she wants to be part of. She has to advertise the merchandise and show that she has dates and is available. Her ultimate goal to be seen by "the" him is crucial. If seen by him often enough, she may make the kill and rope him.

If a more desirable male hookup asks her to a dance and to leave with him, off she goes, it is working, screw the poor escort, what could he expect.

I am not saying that only women do such dastardly things to their partner for the night. Men can drop their dates like hot potatoes and abandon them there alone and to fend for themselves and get home alone or with somebody else. A hot beauty, will she or won't she? That is what blind dates are for, aren't they?

With the introduction of pills and insertive devices, sexual intercourse is expected by all involved.

PLOYS FOR ACTION

Of course, kinky stuff can be good. No matter which partner instigates the change and surprise, it can work wonders. The old humdrum preparation and performance of the sex act, anything new can be exciting and reconstitute one's marriage.

The change of positions – sex toys, etc., can make all of the difference. Do both the male and the female reach a point where they wonder what if? How would that bimbo or stud be in bed? Once finding out of marriage sex, it is difficult to give up and can result in a nasty breakup, no matter how long they have been together.

The problem is that there are many hot pants bimbos out there seeking a fling and since men think of sex every five minutes, they are always ready to go. Throw care, worries and consequences to the wind. Gotta have it!

Man the excitement planning the rendezvous. The worry going forward and escaping afterwards of a safe encounter. Each time a little bit safer and fun to accomplish. All the time involved, knowing full well that their bubble may burst and be found out - discovered.

Now it dawns on the two what a risky – foolish thing to have done. What were they thinking? Too late, paradise lost!

HORMONES RAGING

Lets face it, women like-crave sexual intercourse at times even more than dirty old men and the so called sex-hungry for sex all the time dirty old men.

I have always wondered until recently how a flat out gorgeous babe could be attracted to some of the most disgusting looking men on the planet.

Perhaps they feel that they stand out in his presence and get more looks and appreciation. It is a given that looks are important, but not nearly as important to a woman than the safety of being secure and taken care of with few worries is the most important thing to them. Wealth makes a big difference.

Any man with a large penis is an inducement to wedded bliss. If none of this satisfies a woman, then she can say what Stan said to Ollie, "What a fine mess you've got us into this time, Ollie." Divorce is rampant now here and she can try again. You've made your bed, now lie in it even if not for long.

Buyers remorse is always present for both parties. Sometimes an upcoming go-getter with a future success can be a wise choice for the female, not rich, yet.

Men make stupid choices being all gung-ho for a voluptuous pinhead with a great body and to hell with reality. "Gotta have a "broad" rat now!"

I remember as a youth that one was told that you cannot pry a woman's legs apart and rape her, unless she agrees. Although vice-like strength in her legs being true, the stronger male can usually prevail and satisfy himself. So Rape.

Look out boys, after having consensual sex with her, she can always get sympathy by claiming she was raped. Safety first, know your mark well, be prepared and protect yourself from contracting a venereal disease.

THE CRUELEST CUT OF THEM ALL

I can see why in olden times the sages came up with the cruel practice of circumcision. The foreskin hangs over the head of the penis and at an early age there is some seepage of semen on boys. If not cleaned out daily, it forms a yellow-white cheese under the foreskin. Not a pretty sight and can get pretty rotten smelling if not tended to. The cutting of the foreskin to the back of and exposing the penis head permanently solves that problem and makes the head very tough and takes away much wonderful sensation for the man, back then to prevent disease, maybe would have been okay.

Otherwise, not being circumcised creates loose skin, which rides back and forth and makes for an easy and fun penetration of the vagina.

People living in desert areas had little water and no soap or substitute to use to clean the penis with more modern, bigger city living, water and cleanliness became more accessible and need to continue that barbaric tradition is totally unnecessary anymore. Men do just fine without having it done and more and more doctors are advising not to do that to a boy child. That is my opinion and I stick to it. Stop the cutting! Shower daily!

This tradition surely was not worldwide and some how men lived and went on to father children. Monkey see, monkey do. Use your brain and think about it. Women have been brain washed to fear an uncircumcised penis. Those who have been cut up, don't know the ease of the collapsing foreskin and how well it performs. Misinformation and fear abide in the land.

In Athens Greece, a famous Hollywood actress, who was shacking up with, Howard Hughes, was perched up on a piano and with her legs wide open and sans panties. A Hollywood gossip lady reporter, gasped, "My god, it's a crotch!" It made all of the newsstands. What men don't love to see that?

Beware Of Disease, Ask

This day and age, even more so than in the past, sexual partners may have any number of communicable diseases acquired. Who knows who was at fault, and not even be aware of it.

For the men, only safe thing to do is to choose old maids and when no other women are available, rely on their trusty left hand to masturbate. It is regarded as sacred in some religions.

I wonder if a priest dare to do this as in the Bible they are told to dump their seed on the belly of a harlot?

In a monastery, jail, in war, in the desert, nobody around, why not? Took care of that monster, so there!

There is an old joke-tale of the women who give blow jobs in a whorehouse that spit the cum from their mouths into a bucket and at the end of the day get to drink all of that protein, the one with the most wins.

A blow job going down on, giving head, done well consists of the woman licking-kissing-going around the head of the penis. Next taking the whole erection into her mouth. Lots of juices. Then she starts to suck hard to get the jazz to come out in an orgasm. The closer to ejaculation imminent, she blows hard to send the liquid back and continues to tease the release from coming until he can no longer hold it back and fills her mouth. Her decision whether to swallow it. She usually licks up any spillage running down her chin and all over the lucky guys cock. Universal alternative method of getting it off without the carnal pleasures, not to say that horny male animals can't do both. Don't quit, keep it going-coming. Suck his brains out.

CURRENT GOINGS ON

At this point in time, while driving an auto, walking down a crowded street and in almost every possible situation, imagine a woman-girl without a cell phone glued to their mouths and ears. You can't go far without seeing this going on. What is so important to talk about?

This must be some sort of escape mechanism from reality. What on earth can be so important that she must be connected by the phone to someone-anyone all the time?

I suspect that in her mind it is a status symbol and a cry to look at me. I'm somebody! Someone special, one who has many friends, interests. A business-necessary call? Highly unlikely and pure chauvinism-nonsense and could be a very expensive usage and money wasted.

On top of this new driving distraction, how about women farding, tending to her appearance while speeding along? Eating, drinking, combing, fluffing their hair and adjusting body parts. These activities and the new macho attitude of ladies to be equal to and show hated men how powerful women are. They speed, dart in and out of traffic and anyone of the above mentioned can be an accident waiting to happen! They burn rubber, squeal the tires and pass me in a blur, so there!

I can hardly explain the shock, dismay and disbelief one experiences upon awakening next to a true blond or naturally grey overnight bedded down lady.

It is frightening to look over and see what appears to be an emaciated, pale-ghost like washed out looking supposedly woman. Who is this thing with no discernible eyebrow, -eyelashes and unpleasant looking lips? Disappointed, yes. Scary, yes. Don't think that I could go through this freak show on a regular basis.

WILL THE REAL WOMAN PLEASE STAND UP!

The type of cosmetics, hair care, hair dye colors, use of false eye lids, eye shadings, push up bras, ear rings, things put in the nose, ear, tongue, necklaces, bracelets, rings, ankle chains, painted finger nails and toes, tattoos, shaved armpits and legs, these things can transform an ordinary looking woman into a movie starlit in the eyes of a man who is drinking and make her a desirous conquest. The proper lip gloss applied is a great come on and an invitation to swing with her. It says, "KISS ME! EAT ME!"

I recall in college going through a line of young-sorority girls to be introduced to them. One of my pledge brothers was nasty with his putdown of many of them by shouting loudly, "dark roots", made me consider looking more closely at broads to see what color their hair really is and the color change was done to make her more attractive. Usually so. Our names by the end of the line of being introduced was more often than not, so far off from our real name that there was no way that the girl could ever look you up nor contact you.

I learned an important lesson on how to get a fantastic looking woman being introduced-interviewed-lied to by a sex hungry group of men climbing all over themselves, pressed close to her to get a whack at her and not being very adult like and slobbering with lust, me too.

This one savvy, handsome guy, just stood in plain sight of her and far away and was acting like, what's the big deal? No interest. She couldn't stand his aloofness and had to personally meet him to see if her wiles could interest him and change his mind about her. Worked like a charm as she wanted him and he swaggered out with her on his arm. Clambering all over her like all of the others. Who among them stood out? To win the prize, be different and go slowly.

Men always lose all track with reality when they fall in love. They become giddy and see the woman as being perfect and never has to shit nor puke.

Euphoria In Love

No faults has she. A most ideal desirable mate. On these happy occasions of first telling all of his newly found love, something has to be done right now to bring him back down to earth. A word picture in one's mind can do the trick. Ask him to picture her in the nude, sitting on a commode and splattering the nice white lining with her wet runny diarrhea! Allusion gone. You mean she has to shit? Might even add that she is barfing-puking all over her boobs. The tears will always be upper most on his mind every time he sees and is with her. Bar rag and a change of panties, please. No bloody stuff!

That informative essay brings to mind body odors. We all have them and each sex has distinctive smells and unless one is married and has gotten used to each other. Then one is surprised at the discovery and not used to it yet. Surely uncomfortable with the new essence and ready to eventually look forward to the smell.

Perspiration and lack of cleanliness around a man's scrotum creates a smell unlike any others. Underarm sweat and out-pourings after one has eaten garlic, onions and other things which come out of your skin or your breath, can be a big turn off to either sex. Brushing one's teeth and popping a breath sweetener is a must. We like our own smell, but others may be revolted and aghast.

Now let us explore the most important techniques as the first step to create the best arousal. Women, understandably, do not like to be, just out of the blue, to be mounted, entered and be unexpectedly given fast in and out thrusts by the man.

WHAT WOMEN WANT-DESERVE
IF YOU THINK HER VAGINA IS CLEAN, LICKING, KISSING MUFF DIVING IS OK

Now lets get to the important proper first steps to assure the creation of a possible sure thing to engage in desired sex. Chicks, they crave foreplay.

First of all, if either of you thinks, plan ahead. It can result in a great merging of the bodies and two, happy love birds.

A nice candlelit dinner, a little wine-alcohol to loosen up the libido, a pleasant surrounding, nice bed - what else could be better. Whomsoever created this scenario doesn't matter, as it will charm the panties off of her and you might trip and pole vault onto the bed because of your hard erection. Nice landing. Go for it. By now a little caress of her nipples and they will come out to attention, hard and firm. She will have a flushing of ruby-red sensation, goose bumps and an intense desire to go ahead right now. Another useful prep is to pour sweets or cool whip on her vagina and take your time licking it off. Coitus can't help but be more enjoyable for her and it tastes so good.

If the lady is not too old, her body will self lubricate the area making for comfortable in and out easily. It wouldn't hurt to be sure to apply KY, a product which ensures pleasurable penetration to enhance intimacy. Put some on both you and her.

You could, maybe should, apply KY to the head of your penis and all over it to make you trip more fun, too. If you apply the KY, it gives you an excuse to explore the pussy and to arouse the clitoris. Fun trip for both of you and you will soon be gliding in and out of the Garden of Eden luxuriously and exciting. Oh, just to think of it. Down, big guy. Of course, to return to the original turn on. A long-meaningful kiss on the lips, focusing on her upper lip, sucking the air out of her may create a dizzy euphoria making her almost pass out with fervor. Exploring her tongue with yours (French kissing) and letting your tongue tickle the roof of her mouth is exotic.

Be slow, gentle when massaging her gorgeous boobs. A good way is a surprise diversion of gently touching, rubbing the area between her armpit and the side of her breast. Very sensitive there and a harbinger of good things to be felt on the way to cupping, lifting the boob and sucking on the nipple and even light biting is good. Those beauties were not forgotten and oh, so appreciated.

Licking, kissing all the way down to the promised land is a must for the joy of you both, this has to start the juices flowing. Knowing your lady will inform you in advance if she likes the fantasy of being raped and roughly handled.

All are my hands

Might even be more exciting-different if the man thinks he is raping some other beauty and having his way with her. No surprises - contracts in advance. See there, a new scenario in your head did wonders.

Cuddling, huddling, holding in your arms along with many kisses, thank you's and gentle touching and massaging after an off mount can not be overlooked and practiced.

It's a great life and wonderful experience and don't forget and take it for granted! Wipe her off with wet rag.

Don't these mind pictures drive you crazy? A man may be tempted to stick it to anything that moves. A repairman, traveling salesman may be greeted at the door and his clothes ripped off by the lady of the house.

I have a marvelous memory of being at the end of the bed, deeply imbedded in the pussy and her legs up and over my shoulders. The lips of her snatch were doing exactly that, tightly wrapped around my cock, there was a tremendous vacuum created and an extreme sucking action.

My tool upon excited and rapid thrusting in and out and I knew shortly the climax of an orgasm, when all of a sudden the tight seal between us was broken and the air escaping and being resucked in caused a loud farting-like sound and happily continued until I shot my load. What fun and excitement for the both of us. We collapsed in laughter. Can happen every time and does.

Not me, used no condom protection. Didn't ask her if she had protection. Lucky me, no kid that I know of.

ORGASMS AND RAPE

Having spoken earlier about rape, it reminded me of an era when there were many unsolved rapes and even one girl raped and killed during WWII. The authorities were convinced that they were caused by the large number of servicemen stationed here. They were allowed to wear civilian clothes when off duty and fit right in with the local population.

Our local ladies were alone, with many of their husbands gone serving over seas. Also, their age group of men were mostly there, too. The ladies looking for some needed companionship, naturally hung-out in the local bars and went to well attended dances. It seems to me that a casual meeting between the two, fun seeking groups could explain the huge number increase in reported rapes. Maybe one or more were involved in attacking the women. Left town, out of sight on orders.

My high school health teacher for the boys was very concerned that we may take to raping girls. He said don't do it and go to one of these five or six brothels instead. He gave us the local addresses and said that there were no excuses to do otherwise. No raping!

For me, one of the most pleasurable, exciting things that I can do is to take a hot shower with a handheld sprinkler head with many openings. They put out many strong streams of water and, when directed to my balls and penis, give the glorious sensation of hundreds of tiny pricks of agitation and tickle and create a glorious feeling never before experienced. I hate to ever stop the action, wishing to go on until the hot water ceases. By finishing by spraying with cold water, the ending is glorious. Not quite like having sex, but close to it.

Now let us travel to the anus, rearend, asshole, bung hole, you name it. The derriere-posterior butt seldom seen are rapture, using this hole for fun sex will take a little instruction and good advice. First of all, one should be very generous with an application of KY gel. The wrinkled hole is much smaller than a cunt. Beautiful bottoms protect this hole.

With a hard erection slowly ease the head of the cock into the opening. Very tenderly-slowly ease into the rectum and colon. The women will feel every inch of penetration and it will drive them nuts. They will love it and be anxious for greater penetration. Make her wait, sadistic or not, and then begin furiously plunging in and out to the maximum, there should be some groans and screams of delight. They won't want you to ever quit, but you must withdraw before you blow you load of tiny boys into her ass. Where you dump it is up to you. Know your lady.

Now I come to an examination of the special nomenclature appendages located on mysterious women only. Let's start with her clitoris. Was this just a useless piece of gristle much like one's appendix? At a given moment in the maturization of a baby who became a woman instead of a male baby and it became his penis? Strange left over from the decision making of a child. The bladder holds urine.

Nomenclature

The vulva is a split powder puff, spongy protection for the entrance of the vagina. The labia majora and the labia minora are as named a lip large flap and a lip small flap of skin extending to the interior of the vagina. The pee hole is below as a function to empty the urine from the holding tank, the bladder, through the urethra tube. All of these important genital organs should be cleaned on a regular basis by douching. Women can hide, cover up any bad smelling odors by use of deodorants, perfumes and a variety of preparations specifically designed to cure and lessen any problem eruptions.

It may be years before a boy gets a good look at a girls huge gash-like opening called the vagina. It extends from the lower front below her belly, clear to within a short distance of the anal opening.

Pubic hair grows over the cunt as a girl ages. For a man, the pubic hair grows above his penis and covers his scrotum containing the testicles. The balls are very sensitive and it can be almost immobilizing if they should be grabbed or hit hard.

The idiotically placed prostate on a man is a doughnut shaped thing which supplies added fluids to mix with the testicle discharge to assure that enough is sent into the vagina to properly send the little minute tadpole-like swimmers to try to get to and penetrate the woman's egg and thus start the creation of a child.

In a woman, cervical cancer and breast cancer are most often deadly cancer spots. Men have prostate cancer, colon and testicle cancer most often. I probably don't know anything about this stuff and have left out additional named important parts of the anatomy.

THE PILL CREATED MORE BIMBOS

The pill, which ensures that there will be no babies created from unprotected sex. Upon the widespread availability and the usage, women went wild with glee. The world's their oyster.

Any port in a storm. She can agree and enjoy sex at any place and at anytime. Free at last. Anything goes - nobody can stop me now. I can go on the offensive and lure anyone that I want to romp with me. Throw care to the wind.

This was the start of women coming out of the closet and displaying their true heretofore hidden, secretive nature of wants and desires. From that newly found freedom, we have seen the result of the aggressive, bitchy, controlling and "I am your equal if not better than you" men attitude, the penis envy reduced immeasurably, let it all hang out.

From the day that pill taking begins, there is no more hypocrisy on the part of women and their original hidden cruelty is out in the open and used to reveal their "I'll show you" previously, I appeared naïve, coy and used tricky ploys to appear seductive and capture the poor sap in their planned web of deceit.

Women, now overdo their so-called power and make asses of themselves by overtly throwing previous caution to the wind. Wear no panties, expose their breasts, cuss, drink too much, take drugs, challenge all men wherever and take wild risks. We'll show you! A sorry state of affairs.

A fish?

Being Dainty Trained For Flatulence

I have always been envious of the female gender being sneaky, secretive and for knowing how to squeeze off a fart, slowly and quietly.

This must be one of the things women talk about and instruct each other privately, men seem to be proud of letting go a triple flutter blast out loud most any place. No shame for us.

Of course, men disown the dastardly act which they have unleashed, by pointing at some other saintly person and acting like them, not me!

As we grow older, it is almost impossible to hold in, hold back a thunder blast, with each step out she comes, putt, putt, putt.

Men play games trying to discern what someone ate to create a specific aroma. It is one of our proud achievements and in our minds like issuing out a baby, perhaps. Job well done.

Of course, the farter does not dislike the smell of his own doing, but anybody else's fart, "Katey, bar the doors" and shouting, "Who shit?"

Farting in bed, I assume that I am not alone, one who lifts up the covers, flaps them to expel the smell and gleefully think to oneself, job well done.

This subject, pardon the expression, is not aired publicly in polite societies. Some in my memory, others farts of course, stand out in my memory as to be world beaters. I know who did it, the time, the place and my ugly reaction. Always, how could you?

I guess that women practice opening and closing their cheeks for their assholes and have more control. Practice, practice to be dainty. Squeeze'em off.

Very close friends of mine had a neat wedding. There was much carryings on and the booze flowed.

Finally, the couple departed for their honeymoon quarters and as prescribed, the groom carried his bride over the threshold. First mistake.

Now, this beauty was close up and personal with all of the well wishers for hours and finally could relax. On their way into their honeymoon hide away and in her hubby's arms, she farted. They both collapsed in laughter and were off to a good start in their marriage. There would be no secrets between them, but from the diving-board? Now does one ever tell their children the complete rest of the story? Me, I would have squeezed them off. See, the early dainty training paid off. From that day forward, let them RIP.

Of course, fan like crazy to not overly offend nearby pilgrims.

So much more can be said and I am sure that you can think of many other subjects to discuss about living and interactions between men and women.

After I finish my outburst, I will leave it up to you to fill in the gaps and missing pages.

Early Training

I recall vividly my teen years when buddies were dating a hot babe regularly. He would write sealed notes to his girlfriend and put <u>SWAK </u>on the back of the envelope. It meant, "So want a kiss?" These same steady daters would gossip (see we did it too) that last night, while kissing her and she being distracted, he crawled his hand down inside her panties and plunged fingers into her vagina. No complaints evidently. They called that getting stink finger. Very appropo as we all had the same reaction to a different Odor and smell which we had never encountered before. Several of this gang who squealed on his actions, actually a few years later married his lover.

The phrase "a pile driving ass," the fast piston like thrusts. Do women consider this to be an end of the orgy bonus and liked by all women? Stuff about a lay and getting laid.

It seems to me that at times too rough a jostling is too much and may be out of line. Better ask her before its too late. Since both men and women (who prefer sex in a darkroom) can close their eyes, (women dreaming of their prince charming) and a hunk of a man on top of her and the man has under him and his control a beautiful desirous movie starlet, the two of them can find satisfaction in the act. All in one's mind.

Just kiss her, thank her, hug her and say, "I love you," should get you both off of the hook if it is believable and you can dream on of your lovely conquest.

I don't care about all of the threats of danger to one for cigarette smoking, it is the perfect wind down for me. Smoke a cigar to celebrate, if you got em.

No doubt that recreational sex-fucking, is a universal past time and tension reliever, and so to bed and a good sleep.

Sex Always On Mind

I read one time, that men think of sex once every five minutes of their waking hours. I agree, as it's fun to speculate - dream of some fantastic-ball busting (oh, that hurts) romp with a gorgeous beauty. At night, when I am dreaming about sex, I hate it when the face of one after another beautiful face keeps changing for me. I guess that's OK as I get to have more variety that way.

With the advent of pills to prevent pregnancies, the world has become a horny gal's oyster. They have thrown caution to the wind. Free at last, free at last, now I can screw anyone, anytime that I choose to do so. No regard to where the slugs cock has been before and not knowing if he lied and has a venereal disease. Now she is a carrier and can pass the VD onto many others before she becomes aware that she has a problem. Surely, finding and notifying all of the men in time is almost impossible to achieve and in the meantime he is passing it on to many other unsuspecting claimants.

I remember as a boy when I was swimming nude with my older heroes before they all went to war in WWII. This sexually active braggart was standing on the bank of the dammed up creek, done by them, and it made a nice-deep cool pool to swim in. This guy had this largest swollen cock and balls that I had ever seen. The clap-gonorrhea you name it was rampant even back then. Catching syphilis was even worse if not properly treated. The guy with it may never be able to father healthy children, affecting his brain and maybe causing him to go crazy until his death.

WARNING ON DISEASE

When I was in the army in Japan, my regiment was having an epidemic with up to 50 percent of the 3,000 plus soldiers there infected with a venereal disease. Not me. We had surprise awakenings during the middle of the night. We were herded naked to our latrine and one by one the personnel of my barracks were examined to see who had VD. We were ordered, in front of an examiner, to skin it back (the fore skin). If not circumcised, and to milk it down! Much like squeezing a cow's tit and shooting the milk out. By so doing, if one were infected, a white pus like substance would come out of the head of the penis.

The Japanese people were immune to some diseases which we were not. Red signs over our wash basins warned not to drink the water - contaminated. Many men contracted horrible diseases of which our anti-biotics were useless to cure.

Two commodes in the latrine were designated on big red signs, venereal disease only. Those who had VD were to use them. It is impossible to catch VD from sitting on a toilet and those who had it did not want to be singled out and recognized. Thus, these rarely used, clean water closets, are the ones which I used.

We were like all young men. At that age, we were fearless and didn't believe anything could kill us and nothing can hurt me. That is why your services prefer young boys to do the fighting. Take the orders to charge and no objection from them and blindly charge ahead. It is your duty, God, Duty, Honor, Country.

I stood in a long line in a famous park in Kyoto, Japan to pay for my first blow job, called getting head, by a gook woman, she would bow down, take your erected penis into her mouth and suck and blow it until you had an orgasm in her mouth. Pay first. As I anxiously neared the front of the line, I saw her and she had gobs of cum running out of her mouth and down her chin. In English, she loudly told the guy she had blown, to kiss me. Revolted, I beat a hasty retreat.

There were small openings in the fences surrounding our huge base area. Nightly, several times I was detailed to guard duty on a specific stretch of fencing and was armed with a loaded M1 rifle. We were to yell halt, and capture the many poor people who tried to enter the camp and steal things to sell. I saw one guy who had gotten over the fence, kicked a shell into my M1 and ordered him to halt. He darted back to safety.

Aptly named by us, suck a hatchie Annie, came every night to a secluded stretch of the fence. Many men would pay her to get a blow job through the fence. I guess that no guard reported turned her in.

I told in my first book titled "Noodling and Canoodling Around" one of my friends who was a medical aid man on base. The prostitutes were gathered up monthly and examined for VD. My friend would pick the prettiest, shapeliest gal who turned out safe and clean. He would set her up to live in a place off of the camp and his personal property and his lay. For as little as something like a "T" shirt or a few cigarettes, he had the use of her for a month or until he tired of her. She was cared for and fed well. She probably took needed food to her family days and got many other gifts from him to sell and help her family. I always wondered if ladies nails are clean under their nail polish?

A fixer-upper home

Advantage Of Staying At Home

Women who stay at home and work like hell doing the myriad tasks and chores around the house have all day to think of something to spring upon their husbands first thing upon his coming home from work. She had all day to refine her request out of the blue and to demand an immediate answer or fix of the problem from her tired hubby.

That is probably why some men frequent a local bar to join the others avoiding going straight home after work and having several drinks to fortify himself from the onslaught awaiting him at home. Many pop a beer at home immediately to put the days troubles behind him and to put off the talk-talk rambling on by his wife and daily new demands foisted upon him. There is no time allowed to think over and to evaluate her new requests.

For some men, who always are thinking about having sex and want no interruptions in their quest, the little lady can put a road block on his dreams, by denying him sex until she gets her way. I'm tired -have a headache - you must do so and so first - my way or the highway. You know who wins the stalemate. Putty in her hands, not a pretty picture - c'est la vie - give the devil her due!

No matter how bad the differences between man and wife cool it. No matter how much hate for one another develops between the two of them it is not worth it to harbor a grudge. Get over it, life goes on. Remember forgiveness and love makes the world go round.

ADVICE AND LIFE PREPS

I have a complaint against new mothers. They throw their male boys over their hips to carry like a bag of flour. The kid is spread legged over her bony hip bone and it makes for easy carrying, however, it hurts me to wonder if she is even aware that his tiny testicles are being punished horribly by her unthinking regard for them? I am sure that the baby tries to shrink up the scrotum to try to avoid the pain and who knows what damage is done to him over long run because of this inhuman casual disregard.

Most little girls are dressed in pink and instinctively drawn to and are given dolls to prepare them for motherhood. They play house, have imaginary tea parties, acting out pouring into tiny cups at their first hostess duties at their party. They have many other little girl friends who do the same things and because of left side brain usage learn to talk very early on and my how they can talk. Imitating the adults.

Boys are slow learners to talk and read as they are busy running, fighting, throwing things and doing active things rather than talking about world politics. The boys can't imagine what the little girls find to talk about and being self centered, figure the girls are talking about them.

I think the following cartoon I saw and I'll describe shows the difference between the sexes right on. Apparently, the men and women were at a cocktail party. There was a large group of women on one side of the room gesturing, pointing and mouths all open. The men were all huddled, not talking much, but drinking heavily. There was an impenetrably deep-dark chasm between the two different sexes. Amen. Praise the Lord.

Turn Downs-turn Offs

There's an old saying that you should never go to bed being mad at each other, sage advice. The continuing disagreement can escalate into all out war between the partners and there can be long term hell to pay. Sexual favors can be put on hold. The gap between you can widen and be the start of divorce; tearing up your wedded bliss. The man may find solace in the arms of another woman. She will be such a nice time, no bitching at him nor complaining. She may have her hooks into you and work her ass off to separate you two for good. Who knows what the new, unknown vixen may turn out to be, should you foolishly marry her. Big trouble in river city.

Loo out, there are many evil women out there. They will stick you mit a knife and throw you in a swamp and the mosquitoes will eat you up. Play on actual occurrence experienced by a merchant marine pal on a dock in South America. He was warned that on shore leave that there were evil men out there. I substituted women for men.

Before rushing into a marriage with a hot cutey, who can't get enough sex from you and is easy and can't refuse you. Loo out!

One should be sure to meet the ladies parents, siblings and relatives as you will have to live with them being around forever. Are they all fat, obnoxious people? It may be a fore runner of things to come. Women can lose their lovely shape and get fat in the blink of an eye. Observe their neighborhood, house, autos, interior furnishings. You can continue to bang her, but be prepared to make a hasty exit, if you find any questionable goings on or expectations of you. Loo out!

Choosing A Winner

Of course, you should be aware of whether the chick has an education, any brains or she is an airhead, a flake, a pin head and does she have any talent? Like music, or want to go dancing all of the time? Whom does she know, hang out with? Who has she slept with and had previous affairs with? How many, if any, children does she want? What religion does she prefer? Pay particular attention to her close friends as they will bug you forever if you link up with her. Hard to exclude her coterie of acquaintances.

If you have money and property, you may need a prenuptial agreement. Who knows if this merger will work out and you will live happily here after. Just remember that women have plotted and planned all of their waking moments to latch onto their Mr. Right. They can always shape him, change him, right? Loo out, doesn't work. Don't make any snap decisions just because you like her action in bed. A word to the wise.

Of course, men can be just as devious as a woman. He may not be interested in a long term commitment and just using her for his own pleasure. Be sure to project a man's earning, advancement potential in the future. Does he have a future? You may wind up with a slug and an unhappy life. Ask to see his checkbook, a list of his assets and properties owned. Does he dress well? Who are his close friends and his close associates. Will you live in your present city? Who were his previous conquests? What and where does he go on vacations? Same thing every weekend?

Who in the close family has a history of health problems and whether the family has good genes and long lives? Do check her teeth and any health problems.

You see making a commitment is a serious thing to be carefully considered and checked out, early exodus may save you future heartaches and headaches.

Loo Out!

Women seeking a divorce had better be careful in selecting an attorney to represent them. They can be asked to come up with some serious money for representation. I knew a lecherous dirty old man who took on the task of aiding ladies who had meager money to profer. He would offer to assist them in court for no charge if they would allow him to screw them. As he told it, many did and he scored on them. He bragged on all of his easy lays, Damned gossip.

He was a divorced father himself, also, he was a heavy drinking drunk and not a richly paid money earner. He quite often recited all of the names of the parts of a woman's vagina. Very proud of knowing them all. Genetalia was always on his mind. He mastered hypnosis and would in a bar, in front of our gang, hypnotize a cute girl and leave her with a suggestion, upon her hearing it, he would take her out of the bar and fuck her.

He bragged that once in a jury trial, he stood close to the jury panel and hypnotized a juror, putting her to sleep and resulting in the trial stoppage, mistrial and the jury dismissed. No doubt a sadistic-illegal thing to do and how would one ever know if it is true?

In college, we all knew of a female, pretty girl, who was a nymphomaniac. She had to have sex, anywhere, anytime and couldn't care less what the stud looked like.

We dated working girls and when asked who they were, we said they were Rho Chi Alpha sorority girls. This seemed to pass muster and the girls liked being called sorority girls. You see, they worked at the local RCA plant locally. Hoping to catch a promising young college man with promising careers ahead, they were very generous with sexual favors after being greased well with liquor. Naughty, naughty. Those were the days.

OVER NIGHTERS

Back to my army times. One of my friends came into our room and was all excited after having sex with a local pickup girl. He was amazed and he said she had a huge penis as well as a regular vagina thus a hermaphrodite. One in a million and he got her. I think that she was the one who lay on her back spread eagled and casually eating one grape at a time. She kept up a steady question of him, you no cum yet, Joe? Over and over, just an ordinary day. Something to do.

Another memory that I have wondered about ever since. We (my gang) were all employed for the summer as ground keepers at the best local country club. We had to get there by Trailways bus and that meant that this night we had to catch a bus at 2:30 a.m. to ensure that we would be there by starting work time of 5:00 a.m. to mow the greens for Tuesday lady's day golfing.

We had quite a walk from the highway drop off and we spotted a parked car of late night lovers. As we snuck up on the car, we heard the girl ask the boy what would happen if she got pregnant? He assured her that there was no worry, just piss and it will all come out. Poor baby seemed assured she would be OK after she stepped out of the car and from behind bushes, we watched her piss. Does this really work? Always wondered if she had a baby nine months later?

Another time at that popular sex parking place, we surrounded the car and began rocking it, interrupting their coitus. The guy jumped out furious and lit a match. Holding it up in front of himself, he yelled, I can see you. We fell to the ground for cover, laughing hysterically and he drove off hastily.

All women need is a daily injection. This allows them to feel wanted and needed. The man may slow down, but as often as he is able, is a must do.

Now, what do these mature women gossip about?

WATCHING THE WICKED

Then there was this gorgeous blond whom we knew as Bonny Boobs, her day job was tending a popular bar on the beach in Florida. We liked to pop in there to see her. Literally, see her, as she wore very little clothes and had very revealing figure. She had her own blackboard of men's business cards. She put her payday business card of her previous nights romp. She loved to recount blow by blow what the man did and how he stacked up to others. She came right out and exclaimed that he must have shot a cup full into me. The size of the organism seemed exaggerated to me, but I didn't know and no other woman had ever said that. She felt and knew that it was over for me by feeling warm liquid penetrate her? Maybe so, but fast going, then slack and limp must notify her that it's over, right? She loved to brag. I wonder if she gossiped about it with her close girlfriends? That one's good - avoid him!

I have never been one excited about nor craving to have sodomy. As a boy, we called it corn holing someone. Rear entrance, butt fucking. It seem so dirty in my mind. I worry that the recipient might have runny bowels and all of a sudden a gusher of stinking wet brown stuff would get all over me and coat my penis. Eradicating the odor, tough.

No doubt the small wrinkly anus opening can latch onto one's penis with such a hold that it would be pleasant to have. It might even be fun to do and it has been popular for eons. The woman must feel a pleasure unlike any experience ever felt. Some pressure, touching and massaging body parts previously neglected. I have seen cassettes showing women grimacing, smiling and almost screaming with delight. One must most assuredly withdraw before having an orgasm and shooting inside her. The bible says to dump your seed on the belly of a harlot. One answer, but messy.

IMPORTANT BODY MOVEMENTS

Not being a Don Juan nor a Casanova lover, I am intrigued at all of the various widely used different positions and techniques used by professionals having sex, "slam, bam, thank you ma'am" is a pretty lousy trick to use on a helpless being who is used for your own pleasure only.

Don't men ever consider what the girl enjoys, wants and needs? As a man who has inadvertently had an orgasm from excitement before entering the glory land, I envy those whom can romp for hours on end before climaxing. Surely two, satisfied, but worn out participants - Viagra to the rescue.

I see that a finger injected in a woman's asshole, during the sex act, can create a pleasurable sensation and feeling for a woman. Don't lick your finger. If she is top mounted riding up and down on your erection, she will love the surprise if you reach around behind her and slap her ass hard. A nice distraction, an anus surprise.

Besides those bobbing boobs are a sight to behold. You may be able to grab them, kiss them and fondle them if she bows down far enough, all of these antics may be conducive to make you be inspired and to drive harder.

Such an enjoyable, exciting, face to face, interesting and simple linking of two writhing bodies. It's a shame that one has to go to so much pleading, plotting and advance planning to insure this wonderful sporty action.

The terms used to describe sexual intercourse for such a marvelous exercise liked by both parties is out of place and disgusting in its usage.

When some bastard in disgust with me or something which I have done yells "fuck you", he thinks he has gotten even or even one upped me. He has hurled the ultimate curse phrase at me. Au contraire, mon ami. This supposed vulgarity just shows his lack of intelligence and use of really hard hitting language and lack of anything else to say.

Double Entendre

No victory for you pin head! I walk away from him with a feigned frown on my face when looking at him and a smile when turned and walking away from him. Inside, I have a warm happy feeling to think that he has wished me to get fucked. How nice of him. If he only knew that this outburst only evokes pleasant memories for me.

Where the word fuck came from and how the phrase is supposed to upset one, escapes me, it is a most simple expression and an easy way to say that you had sexual intercourse. Nice thoughts created ordinarily. I admit that I use some form of it almost daily and work it into my thoughts and expressions often in a discrete way scanning the area before blurting out.

The degrading appellations in describing a woman's wonderful vagina is an attempt to let the macho men around that I can say, cunt, box, snatch, twat and other euphemisms to describe her hole. I think I like to think of it as pussy best.

Boys dream of that gorgeous opening (their private dumping ground) and attach their own pet name for it in order to make them to feel macho. Men dream about screwing, another name for it which would be extremely painful if their cock actually whirled and screwed, thus saying screwing.

Women are permanently programmed to produce a certain number of their eggs in their lifetime. Men continue to produce sperm by the millions even while shooting a bunch into a women. In his life, a man makes so many possible babies, if all could penetrate a female egg, that he could himself repopulate the earth.

You must have noticed that I don't, haven't used the worst curse word known to man. There is no way any man will allow another man to call him a mother f****'r.

The insinuation will surely bring out the worst of repercussions to the sayer. He will face retribution which may cause bodily harm to him and possibly the both of them.

One's mother is sacred and off limits. Being called a bastard is fighting words, as women care for and raise their children and have the most influence over them. The mothers are all mentioned by the kids when they are being interviewed. It is always, "Hi Mom." What would we do without them? What would life be like if they abandoned us? Any bad things said about our mothers are fighting words.

Dictionary definition of bitch. Used for a promiscuous woman, a malicious, bad tempered, or aggressive woman, anything especially unpleasant or difficult. Also, a manner of behavior and spitefulness or angriness toward another.

It is hard for one to not bitch or complain about some things or at someone daily. When referring to a woman, surely one of the ultimate judgments. Be aware that when a man is called a son of bitch, he may react angrily and be prompted to take action and do something rash.

49

MORE DEFINITIONS

I thought that it was finally the time to use the proper term of expelling ejaculating sperm. It is an orgasm. The amazing sensation created by such a strong release of the little boogers held back for so long.

Now I want to give my impression of the mostly American men's obsession on a woman's boobs, teats, tits, enlarged sweat glands. You name them. Bosoms accepted.

No doubt that I am taken aback and almost breathless upon seeing a matching set of beautiful breasts on a woman as part of an exceptional accompanying desirable body. I wish that the whole body was mine alone to play with.

Of course, the naked babes silky pubic hair covering her pussy unleashes and triggers wants and long, shapely gams, legs an immense turn on.

I wonder what it is that causes the general wish to be your head completely smothered in the cleavage. To me the bigger, too large tits are ridiculous and disgusting to look at. Knowing that large honkers, knockers, cans, boobs, are what attracts some men and being unhappy with their "B" size, women race out and spend big money to have them enlarged. Trouble about to happen. Don't they know, have never seen an older woman who had big flopping sacks, now has them deflate and dangle down below her belly button. Not a pretty sight.

The Europeans look aghast with wonder at the stupid, ugly Americans for paying so much attention to women's tits and nude body. Nudity is expected and accepted and no fuss made over it. They show no reaction upon their stumbling upon a nude gal sunning on a beach and many times, on a walk along the cliffs, along the Atlantic, from above one sees lovers nude and going at it in a cozy cove. I act in front of them that nothing is going on and an everyday sight and occurrence for me. One last backwards glance as we move on. Are they doing the Australian Kangaroo Hop? Wow!

Of course, in polite society there is fornication – a voluntary sexual intercourse engaged in by a man, especially by an unmarried man.

There is a whole lot of fornication going on. With an unmarried woman by voluntary sexual intercourse between the two parties. If one party is married to another other than their married person involved it is called adultery. Which is unlawful sexual intercourse.

Both fornication and adultery are used interchangeably to describe the whoopee going on.

Thus, it is an activity agreed to by both parties and at the climax of the union and while they both are enjoying the frolic, the two terms are not primary as a worry between either person.

It can be rape if proven not to be conceptual and loo out, either participant can accuse the other of having been raped. Oh, the chances that we take for a fun romp in the hay. The next thing you know, they'll be smoking, drinking and taking drugs.

Vive La French

In France we all have heard that they have a blasé attitude about sex. Just a normal thing to participate in. The long siesta type lunch breaks, allows all men to have a regular hump – mistress and a leisurely "nooner". The wives know and accept this to be going on and are not averse to having an outside lover themselves. Very mature, very French. Almost makes one to want to become a Muslim martyr, die and have 72 virgins to use in paradise. I'd be tempted, too, to jump on the band wagon. If I thought that to be true. Oh, my aching back!

Love is never having to say good-bye. How's that working for you? (Dr. Phil)

Foreplay is the problem most women have with men. They seldom get the satisfaction of a slow, gentle arousal. It is so essential to having a successful union and a satisfied female mate.

Both parties know that it is coming and going to happen. Jumping on and starting to furiously bang away is a sure loser. She feels that she is just your object to be used. Can't be good for you.

Of course, if you are paying a trick for it, plunge ahead, never see her again. It's your call and your money. Enjoy, do what you want, she's only an object and not to worry about technique nor whether she is satisfied. Only a job for her. No matter.

Be sure to get a check up after to be sure you got no VD. We can only hope that the harlot protects her chosen profession, douches and has regular exams as well.

I admit, that me personally, have not been too smart when it comes to relationships with women. I've always been blind and in love with being in love. I see no obvious faults with the current babe under me. I have a history of becoming aware at a much later date, that hey, this broad is bad, no good for me, and run, don't just slink away. Instead of grey matter for brains, she has pulverized maggots in there. Maybe, me too at the moment fun of it all.

A Lady of the Night

WHY DO THEY DO IT?

Some women are inordinately proud of their looks, their bodies and being nice looking.

Why is this evident with all of the beautiful, cute, attractive, interesting show it all, do it all for money pin-up girls and women who appear in pornographic videos? These honeys are not afraid to allow themselves to be photographed being used as dumping grounds for men with humongous sexual organs and appearing to relish and enjoy the romp?

It must be that in their pea picking, little brains, they fantasize being owned by handsome, rich, powerful men and think that by doing so, it will come to fruition. Obviously, an ego trip for both the male and the female. Satisfied to flaunt their looks at me and see what I have got and to think I'm better than you.

What kind of to be desired parents will these people make? There is no doubt, that once exposed like they have been, that it will always haunt them and be used against them forever.

I guess that being asked to perform in public is so flattering, that they just relent and go for it. Worldwide, the pornographic industry is robust and flourishing. There are big bucks available to and for the poor and ignorant and their owners.

Obviously, these folks are not religious and do not believe in any religion. Such a sad state of affairs and meaningless life for them.

I Backed Out Of Marriage Nine Times

As I look back, I thank goodness in the past not to commit myself to a permanent relationship, especially several whom I was the last to know that they had been putting out to all of my close friends. Man, would they have laughed at me and I would have been forever called a sucker. Just couldn't abide - handle that!

As the old adage goes, women, you can't live with them or without them. Security is all that they want and they are looking for. Whom can you trust? Just don't marry a slut.

Women are indeed a blessing for all mankind. They provide a steadying influence on your whole life and your family. God bless them for always being there in good times and bad like a rock to be depended upon.

Men should be eternally grateful for their hard work and their sacrifices for you and your family.

The opposite can be true at one point in time with the relationship between mother and daughter. Since the mom has been there, done that, she tries to shield the girl from making the same mistakes. The young girl in her teens has her hormones raging. She is anxious to break the bonds and be free of all of the regimentation rules and continual criticism. She wants absolute freedom to go to exciting places and participate in all banned activities. Hot pants causes her to want unrestricted sex, being able to experiment with booze and drugs. Smoke up a storm.

Her mature brain has not been developed yet and to have the ability to make sound decisions and to be sensible about things. She might be attracted to an older man, her male companions are so immature and she thinks that she is so mature. The older guy is so cool, has a large cock and constantly soothes her urges. This foray may turn out to be disastrous for her if she becomes pregnant and has a baby to raise at her age, he would be long gone. Talk about trouble.

Later in life, when she is happy and has her own kids, she realizes her old man was right and thankful, goes back to him.

IS THIS TRIP REALLY NECESSARY?
A MARRIAGE COMMITMENT IS SERIOUS BUSINESS

There are many married couples no matter how hard they try, can't conceive a child.

There are many married couples where one or the other of the pair does not want any children and seem to be able to be satisfied in the present. May be a permanent situation not having any kids.

The worst of scenarios are the numerous divorces now a days and the children are the ones who are left out of having both parents to guide and to raise them.

Quite often, both divorced people remarry and often to another divorced person with their own children and mixing of the two groups of children can also lead to a dysfunctional family outcome.

Then there are the marrieds who have nothing but heartaches and headaches with nonconformist, radical, trouble making of their youngsters.

Sometimes a divorce is a good thing where the man and the woman are continually at odds and fighting in front of their children. Many of the battered women choose to remain in these bad arrangements, rather than to divorce, and who suffers because of this madness?

I am disgusted to see more and more interracial marriages and shown on TV all of the time as being alright and accepted. The different colored kids are branded for life and will never completely be accepted.

Not marrying, staying single is not all bad.

Youth And The Parents

Boys harbor a distinct dislike for their old man, too. Especially during their teenage years. Pop knows all of the tricks, lies and possibilities that the son is going through. Having huge hard-on erections at any and inopportune times. Whole lot of jacking-off masturbating thinking of a beauty or looking at naked women's pictures in magazines or a pornographic TV stimulator, why are the girls so mean and won't put out? Then as the boy ages, he has an epiphany and wonders how did dad get so smart so fast?

One can guess - estimate approximately what they might look like should they reach their father's age. Women can as well and if mom has become obese and untidy, they can if they want to take steps right now not to fall into that trap.

Girls have it the hardest, as the father is mean and hell bent to try to keep her from allowing her panties to be pulled off and get a good screwing. She is always questioned deeply as to whom she was with, where they went and why she was late past her assigned time to come home. Passionate necking, having hands groping her all over and if not all the way - stink fingered.

It is critical that the parents are eagle-eyed and closely monitor the poor, hot young girl. Check both for the smell of liquor on their breath, especially the boy. Now with crack, marijuana and other drug use, their stability and demeanor is a sure clue that they are in to it.

An after thought, before I forget, a full, ruby red lower lip on a woman is in vogue, and no doubt is most appealing and desirous. Women recognize this to be true, and if cheated when lips were handed out, can have collagen inserted into the lips and change their look dramatically for the better. There are few women who have what they were originally dealt today. Those her boobs?

I don't necessarily recommend that you require the girl to take off her panties for an eye exam and smell test. The act of threatening her with such an inspection should be enough to warn her and be careful to change her ways.

It is important to closely monitor whom her friends are and nip in the bud any possible unsavory alliances she may have. Known trouble makers with a history of problems should be avoided at all cost. Early intervention can save many future heartaches. Be firm and say, "you're outta there" and "no more."

Parents should examine the boy and the girl's bedrooms daily. The children assume that you are too dumb to discover their hiding places where they have squirled away guns, drugs, condoms and sexual paraphernalia. A stitch in time, saves nine. Do yourself a favor and do it.

You know that one rotten apple can spoil a whole hamper full of apples. Just little things detected in advance may curtail a big problem later on.

Don't let either sex get involved in gang like activities. A strong gang leader can convince, insist that their members must go along with their orders. This companionship can force your kids into all kinds of illegal and dangerous situations.

A word to the wise, talk to and question your kids and be aware of what they are doing. Don't just lecture, talk to them face to face and for God's sake, listen to them.

A safe saying, Shit Happens!

Make it a point to lighten up on your wishes to have sex with your partner. Jokingly, ask your wife if she would like to play hide the weeny? How about telling her the story of two lost travelers coming upon two lovers having sex and asking them, how far is the Old Log Inn?

If you have a son, you have just one boy to worry about. If you have a daughter, you have all of the boys in town to worry about.

There is always a chance that your daughter may turn out to be one of the following:

A Prostitute
A Slut
A Trollop
A Hooker
A Tart
A Tramp
A Shrew
A Bitch
A Whore
A Harlot
A Chippy
A Wench
A Loose woman, Bimbo, a Hussy

It is no wonder that parents, both fathers and mothers have big worries as to what a daughter is into and who might be into her. Little vixens can be nightmares for their parents. Might lead to drink. A bitch in heat, you can bet that she'll be had.

She may resort to doing tricks or just open up to any or anyone for the sport of fun of it.

Yearning-dreaming

OK, so maybe I do think of sex every five minutes the thoughts and wishes to have wild sex with some raving, young beauty is with me constantly. I wonder what it would be like to make it with so and so? Right?

The scantily clad honeys on TV, in ads and movies on TV keeps one permanently aroused. Victoria Secrets gorgeous models and skimpy-come hither bras and bandaids for panties should be outlawed, but I hope not.

It is highly unlikely that one would run into an outstanding beautiful prize locally, I would be speechless, eyes bug out, freeze in place and make an ass of myself. Scared half to death, more than likely I would run away. I'd keep reassuring myself and saying, nothing's going-on. It must be all done with mirrors. Lord help me! Some sort of a vision and I wasn't even drunk. Vamps, flirts, seducers, easy pickings, me.

There is nothing worse than going down the line to select the one which you choose to pay to fuck in a bawdy house. They all give you the come on look and hurt look if you pass on her. Usually just get it over and point at one.

She leads you to her private operating room and in the blink of an eye has disrobed her scanty see through outfit and is spread eagled on the bed expecting your entrance. I hate to see the pictures of her children on her dresser. Well, she's providing well for them. Now where do I put all of my clothes and have to worry about my wallet? It's just a bad start.

HAVANA PRE CASTRO

I just suddenly, ponder whether she is clean and what VD I might be getting? Hopefully, her profession necessitates that she is careful of herself and only has to worry about the asshole paying to have his ashes hauled. Lotta KY gotta be used and baby powder helps a good perfume takes one's mind off whether she is beautiful and stacked or not. Of course, no kissing!

If there is any conversation at all, it usually centers around her next big bucks kill at some upcoming convention. Just can't bring myself to kiss her. The young, unmarried beauties could make for a neat wife, but I would be afraid to leave her alone for any period of time as the easy money available would give her some secret walking around bread and give her ideas.

In a famous, neat whorehouse in Havana, Cuba (pre Castro) after doing my duty and on the way out, the madam tried to get me to glom on to another one for more of a romp. She led me by the huge throng gathered and for a hefty price, one could watch "superman" stick his 15" long penis up to the hilt in some appreciative subject. I saw this monstrosity on the guy. Don't have any idea what his face looked like for some reason.

There are so many self pleasuring devices available today that superman may just have had a strap on size enhancer. Too good to be true? Then it was. My lustful buddies and I visited a famous liquor company and continued to be half loaded, no sleep to be mentioned because of excitement and something in the air. What a shame that not available to us for all of these years. We spent a lot of time in the Sans Souci nightclub and Mafia gaming place. The Copacabana same attraction only better. Huge see through fiberglass high arch with outstanding beauties crossing over like in the movies, good music-entertainment.

Unheard of for me, I sat transfixed looking at these almost nude show girls and didn't even take a sip of my expensive drink. Must have been a great show!

Where is all of this stuff welling up and coming from? Most of these things are not discussed in polite circles. Of course the readers have seen and done much worse things in their lifetimes. I am sure that when ladies gossip, they reveal just as dirty secrets to one another and most likely would blow me away, everyone, is doing it, doing it. The song verse so true.

I admit that I glom onto others relating exploits and am prone to incorporate some things as if I were the doer. It is easy for me to substitute expando me into a (ribald knee slapper).

Does any of this strike a bell with like the Hollywood lifestyle? It seems to me to be just normal carryings on to me. There will always be those who profess, oh, I didn't know that? Oh, my, isn't that awful? Watch out for these people who full well know what really goes on, but liars that they are, feign ignorance. Dead give away.

Oops, it's pee time in Orange, New Jersey. I had to drain the monster and now I'm back. Wipe yourselves off and change your undies, please.

Art Class – I added the cigarette

Like everything else in life situations, I will think later and regret not saying something else. Still the cruelest part of life saying "If only!" Not enough banging and plowing!

As I said earlier, I'm sure that those of you who have stuck with me this far. You have had time to recall the things recaptured of your own personal memories of your sexual romps and not all of them are not pretty to remember. However, your former experimental indiscretions may have led to vivid discoveries for you. Hurting another or not doing so and just full speed ahead. There are still many chances ahead to be taken for us all. Here's looking at you, kid.

I am aware of many elderly couples marrying for the nth time if only for the satisfaction of companionship.

Romping In Mexico

Me and a good friend, drove my car for a visit to a friend who lived in Monterrey, Mexico. We didn't know at first how to contact him so we checked into a nice hotel. The rates were just peanuts.

We dined there that evening and had steaks and all the trimmings and wine. Cost, $1.69. A mariachi band came to our table to play for us. Discovered heaven.

Another day, after making the local connection, he drove my car to a wild cantina where locals carried guns and when excited and having fun, would shoot the guns in the air and many bullet holes in the ceiling. Don't let them know you are gringos!

We went to a local bawdy house and after paying the madam, settled down with our lovelies for an all nighter. We ordered drinks on the phone and they were delivered on a lazy susan in the wall. Just one opening to the inside with the drinks. We were starting to work over our dates, when one of the tarts said our hour was almost up. We were thrown out as we had not paid for all night.

On another occasion, we went down Marco Polo Street to a house nicknamed the Marco Polo. Our friend knocked on the door and a speak easy sliding slot opened in the door and knowing our friend, we went in. Now this place on the interior was amazing tiered table seating, a professional band playing all special arrangements and very good.

The girls were all over us and one was our friend's fav. We got two other luscious babes and for 100 pesos each bailed them out for a whole day. Great time and we ate and my friend drove us all in my convert towards Durango. We didn't have the time to drive over the mountains on a long dangerous trip to Mexico City.

I had to pay some kid to guard my car whenever we walked away to shop, eat or sightsee. Monterrey was inundated by Texans on weekends. I saw a former older doctor from Indiana, who divorced his wife and moved there as it is so much fun and inexpensive. I didn't hail him as he had a lovely on each arm. What a way to go. Golden years retirement, my ass.

We spent three nights in New Orleans on the way home hearing the great jazz music sounds and of course, came down with Montezuma's revenge. Not fun. One night at jazz spots in Memphis, Tennessee and home after one of the all time great trips. Toss up between Mexico and Cuba.

Oops, look now who has been bragging and gossiping. At least the first time that I have made a confession on the Mexican romp. Ole!

I admit that I have told a select group of my friends previously an expanded, revealing, in depth of our adventures of what really transpired.

We wet our whistles and those luscious bodies are still in my wet dreams. If any like them come here as illegals, I would be tempted to take them in and monitor them among other things. A safe port in a storm. Naughty, naughty, shame on me.

Nothings going on. Who knew? Looked clean to me. Just a little something extra to satisfy me and to keep this adventure going on.

As an after thought of the act of passing gas. Both sexes as we grow older notice that we cannot restrain the leakage and go putt, putt, putt with every step that we take. More benefits of the golden years.

EATING AND DRINKING

Our friend, who was in medical school at the University of Nuevo Leone, lived in a boarding house close to the campus in Monterrey, Mexico.

His landlady, insisted that he invite us to dine at her home. All three of us went and were seated at a wonderfully prepared table.

The first course (explanation later) was wine, char boiled steak, French fries and salad. There were heaping servings. We were filled to the brim.

Now the answer, there was a second course. She said, now you eat a Mexican meal. Where to put it? It too was delicious and so well prepared. Every Mexican delicacy, you name it. We ate slower and slower and noting this, she kept saying in English, "You no like?" We ate on and on and I swear that I never ate so much in my lifetime-could hardly walk.

Speaking of gluttony, me and my friend stayed at the Super Anfa motel - very modern with a great swimming pool. We went in while our friend was in classes. We began to drink. We asked for a menu of drinks and told the bartender to start with #1 and run the whole menu. We ran through all that were offered and our friend joined us when we were at Manhattan, Margarita, Martini and Pulche.

Again must have been some sort of world record. Of course, Corona beers made in Monterrey. Please don't tell any body about his. Lucky I can remember what we did. Our college training paid off.

All drinks were served to us in the pool. Margarita anyone?

We All Want To Be Loved

The need to care for someone and to liked and cared for and to be loved is a powerful aphrodisiacs for us all. We have a reason to live on and share our memories together. Since father time is relentless, I say what a way to go.

Okay, let's explore some of the common usages of the word fuck, to fuck, as a word for carnal copulation, to screw, intercourse, sleep with someone, have your way with her and I am sure that you all have your pet sayings to ram it home, lay her and on and on. Nice thing, ain't it?

Then why does someone say fuck you in order to put you down, show you up and how mad they are at you? It is such a lovely union, that is foolish to think that you are hurting someone with that expletive. I'm sure that you have your own way of spouting off with the use of the word fuck.

Now let's get down to the nitty gritty of the limitless number of places, techniques and other ways for two willing partners to join their sexual organs. The old standby is the minister's position with he on top of her. A pillow under her ass to elevate her pussy to enter hands free at the end of a bed. Her legs over your shoulders is fun. Standing up, facing each other and the males hands clasping her ass to assist in and out motion. Face to face in bed with her one leg raised over you. Gives easy access to her boobs and her lips. One can determine how you are doing by seeing her expression and appreciate any groans or screams of delight hopefully.

Cock, prick, dong, penis, divining rod, whatever its called depends upon what was done to it. The head of the cock that has been circumcised, gets hard skinned, tough and is used as a battering ram, being pointed on the end and oval shaped in the back which is larger than the rest of the penis to gain entrance to the vagina. Those men who are lucky enough to have escaped this barbarity.

Be Aware Who Is Watching

Back to surprising places fucking is going on. One day, years ago, I was in the bar room of the Yankee Clipper Hotel in Fort Lauderdale, Florida. There was a huge, strong glass over-looking the swimming pool there. It was below the surface of the pool and the few swimming were not immediately aware that they could be seen and watched.

This day, a young newlywed couple swimming and horny for each other, took off their bottom bathing trunks and started copulating in full view of the drinkers at the bar. Shouts of glee and gulping toasts to the two as they went at it. The word quickly got around and men from across the street came running and soon the room was packed with ogling, lecherous males with erections. What fun. Sperm cum was floating next to their bodies. I think that I went back there quite often as the bartender, whom I knew, said that it is a good show and happens quite often. That was a real keeper. I got a big laugh when I asked for a bar rag and a change of shorts. Nothing like having a nooner.

ALRIGHT, WHO'S THE GOSSIP NOW? These revelations are not things which ordinarily come up in conversations with my male pals. Surely the women gossip even more in depth than I have. Wouldn't you like to know?

Love Nests

Other fun places to rip off a piece of ass are an impromptu connection on the kitchen table, billiard table, sofa, floor, in backseats of cars, in the shower, out of doors, in the tub, hot tub, on ocean cruises, hotel rooms, boats of any kind, hammocks, on hay rides and camping out anywhere. See you can be horny any place. How about like I said, in a pool, a lake, and ocean? Give it a bloody go. Make love, have sex, not war. Oops, I hear some heavy panting in the upper galleries of a movie theater and popcorn, too. Be sure to clean up the kitchen table.

Once on a lunch break, I wandered around a wooded local park along the river. Sure enough couples were having quick nooners. Their dessert out in the open spaces.

I usually get a look of, I wonder, when I excuse myself and say that I have to drain the monster? At least it sometimes get the chick to thinking of what might be waiting for her later in the evening. Lost a bunch that way, appearing too crude in their eyes, win some, lose some! C'est la vie!

Another truism is that everyone, all ages, piss in the swimming pools, but from the diving board? We know where you're going, shouted in unison on way to the water closet in a night club. Then all shouting, did everything come out alright upon your return? Either go through the harassment or stay put and leak in your pants.

Which brings me to ask the question of how do women, now trying to be men and wearing long pants, ever get them and their panties down in time always? We just whip it out, splatter all over and drip on the floor, making a problem for the next guy taking a shit as his pants down can get a soaking. Bodily functions can cause problems and take some careful advance planning. Women have to line up to get into the limited stalls available for them as never enough available. We men, in a panic, turn the water on in a wash basin and flush away.

CHILD BEARING

Don't try to ask me to try to understand what a woman goes through carrying, nourishing, and finally, agonizingly delivering a healthy child. Men, we got it made. We hop out of bed, if we still have hair, run a comb through and be seated to be waited up on to a fine breakfast.

No wonder our ladies who stay, work at home, lounge around all day with nothing on, but a bathrobe. This tends to forestall the tedious task ahead of them to make themselves presentable for all to see. Many working single girls, shack up all night and have to get from their rendezvous and home, do their toilette, change their undies and race off for another day of work. Gossip could enter the picture here amongst the other high lifers.

How do they do it? The women menstruating times must be hectic and who can blame them for being grumpy? What you see is what you get. It is amazing what all they have to go through. Choosing a matching ensemble to wear every day. Hair, cosmetics, perfumes, underarm deodorants and all of the above. No wonder they are seldom on time to go any place. No thank you, I'll pass.

As when Lady Godiva rides side saddle bare assed naked, the side where both of her legs are exposes her entrance to the Garden of Eden and those on that side are indeed lucky and can yell, hooray for our side. Better to have lived and loved, than never to have loved at all. We men wouldn't be here at all without our loving female mothers.

Kudos to all women kind, gossipy and men were not meant to ever understand them. Tell 'em where you got it. Whatever that means?

REPRO SYSTEMS

Stay with me as I ramble on.

I had to consult a medical dictionary to acquaint myself with a woman's reproductive system. Of course, we start with the vagina itself. Front on from its top, we have the clitoris. Going-down we find the vulva. Upon entering the cavity, we find the labia majora and the labia minora and then enter the cervical cavity. No idea how to locate the "G" spot to assure bigger assured orgasms. On to the uterus from the cervical cavity. There is the endometrium, the two fallopian tubes leading to the separated ovaries. Forget the bladder and pee pee hole.

I am not sure that all women can name all of these appendages. Surely, very few men other than doctors. To most men, these remain secrets and discussed at length only between women.

Yadda, yadda, yadda. Blah, blah, blah. Let's talk about sports-our expertise.

In conclusion, women have such an amazing group of necessary apparatus to be aware of and to care for in order to keep them all operating perfectly in order to assure that they can create a human baby. It must be wonderful relief for them to end menstruation and relax and enjoy the rest of her life after menopause and getting more boning.

We love them for their motherly instinct of sharing and caring for all concerned. Of course, we will never understand them and their belief in hunches, innate ability to sense-see through-know in advance-we call it intuition.

Gotta love our gals.

PRESSING ON

Oh, to hell with it, the damage has been done, so why not press on and dig myself into a deeper hole?

I have undoubtedly ruffled some feathers by being so outspoken on my ideas and what we have here and why. That was the title of my third book. Read it, you'll like it.

I'm sure that both sexes will have something to say about this book and what I have said.

Men don't ordinarily open up to one another like our lady friends do with one another. Men talk as briefly on the phone as possible and les femmes gossip for hours on end. The Lord only knows what they find to talk about. Men can lie, expand and exaggerate trysts.

One rarely gets to open up and to expound his thoughts and version of happenings and his ideas.

I hope that the picture of sculptures of the naked ladies caught your eye and your interest in the book even better, I hope that you read it and learn from it. I know that I did. Maybe, my friends were right in telling me to shut up. Being from Indiana, it fit right in with many, loud mouth Hoosiers.

Turn about is fair play and I have exaggerated body parts on my male sculpts and realize that we are hideously ugly compared to a shapely woman. If I were younger, I'd be all over her like a wet blanket. I'd jump your bones like a crazy rapist. As I said in my former books – "Ho, ho, ho, it's nice to be young."

The kids now a days may not realize how good they have it, but we dirty old men know it to be true and say it constantly. The horrible thought comes to mind again, if only! That means a hard-stiff erection of the magic wand, weeny, cock, prick, penis, pecker, dong or any other pet name given for it. Viagra sustaining power scares me. But what a way to go, in the saddle. No boots on.

UGLY MEN

Again, I say that some of my male sculptures are of neanderthal types with enormous pee pipes and would not only be desired by the women, but we poor undersized men would think, if only, too!

This reminds me of a guy that I roomed with in the army. After getting to know someone better, to show that he is accepted and liked by the group, we gave them a nickname which stuck whether he liked it or not.

This particular guy came to mind as being abnormally well hung in that department. I envied him and couldn't help but think how lucky he was and if only. He was a thin, one could say skinny kid, probably only five foot six inches tall and not very muscular nor heavy. His penis hung maybe three or four inches below his balls while limp. What a hero. We called him "schlong."

He would smile back and say nothing when we called him that, just quietly acknowledging his superiority over us all. I hope that he made the most of it's use and finally tired of continuous use on many babes. He would have left a horde of unhappy gals when he finally settled down and married. See, I wished a great happy life for him, if only!

I just caught a day time advertisement-trailer on TV about an upcoming new series to be televised. The star heroine young bitch has a dirty mouth and will be a big hit with the young crowd. She loudly included some sort of the word, fuck on air to introduce herself. I know that women gossiping with their sisters have vile, dirty, salty lingo even more than men, but from the diving board?

I guess that I shouldn't be surprised as it is common place on HBO like the Sopranos, Sex and the City, etc. and now on old line major TV stations, wow! The really young'uns will find it no matter if shown late in primetime. I sort of wish that I had all of these goodies growing up, or do I? If only again.

REAR ENTRANCES

At this point in time, I feel a compulsion to relate some observations about anal sex.

Women seem to act as if they are not always sure that they like the action, but perhaps they really do like it.

Women have many women friends and it is only logical that they can prefer their close association with women. Women understand their own bodies much better than men do. It is only understandable that they should prefer to have another woman to give them pleasant and to always given, pre-sexual encounter foreplay.

With all kinds of strap-on gadgets available, the two women can have the best of all worlds sans an actual male. No wonder so many choose to be in a lesbian relationship.

Now, let's admit it, the men prefer male companionship. The homosexual link up offers them true love and understanding between the two partners.

Upon having a finger wave examination of the male prostate, one often experiences a small orgasm from the searching massage there of. Thus, a male thrusting his penis in and out of one's tight ass hole, can create an orgasm for both of them simultaneously. No wonder many prefer this life rather than with a woman whom he can never understand.

Both sexes have more in common with their own sex than with the opposite sex. Those who can't abide the difference between the two sexes and opt to go with their same sex.

Now, with artificial insemination, women do not need to have a man to impregnate them. The women tend to live longer than the man and those who were married inherit the estate and control more money than their male counter parts do.

Loo out, there is many evil men out there who will try to take the money away from you!

BIRTH RIGHTS

In our society, lesbians, women lovers, and homosexuals, men lovers, are called gays and ferries. The men are considered to be swishy for the way that they sway while walking. Usually they have a limp hand shake and in conversation seem to have a more female like voice. They are loved by heterosexual women and accepted as close friends. One of the two men or women is in charge and control of the other submissive one who adores him or her for their strength.

Both of these two, considered outsider-strange groups of lovers, express their feelings out in the open by holding hands and hugging and kissing one another. They are proud of their actions and show no shame for doing so, thus flaunting their gayness. Called fruits and queers often.

The lesbian women act exactly like the men and one of the women is head of their family and is referred to as the butch, head honcho or a dyke.

All young boys, because of hanging around mostly in gangs of male pals, at some time wonder if they are gay and set out to punish gays by beating them up. They may still have doubts until they fall in love with a girl, abandon being with their friends and get married. Then associate with other marrieds.

Who knows why women gravitate to other women. Is it fear of men and being comfortable taking orders from a forward, pushy, leader-type woman?

Both groups are usually very intelligent and make good livings. I can't fault either one and they don't bother. An emphatic "No" is all that is needed. Not me. Not interested, their loss. Ha!

THE ENEMY

The liberal press, TV, anti religion movie industry, sectarian adherents and the ACLU will scream freedom of the press and fight to the death to allow all vulgar speech to be come common place. The young crumb crunchers will say, "See it is okay to use dirty cuss words!" Wake up America! Unite!

I used to wonder why little girls love to ride horse back so much? A simple, logical answer is the rubbing, caressing feeling of the undulation of the saddle on their clitoris and vulva. An anonymous outside object pleasuring them. Right on!

The egg heads who get huge government hand outs to study such important things have come up with the answer as to how the thin hymen is breached most often. Not by men getting her cherrie as often as we used to pray for. Seems that having sex for the first time doesn't always do the job nor tell the answer where, how and when it is punctured. Now wasn't that worth discovering? Your money.

OK, gone, who was the slob who took it? Crazy gals are now having surgery to replace the hymen to please their permanent first time grabber. Whom do you trust?

Venerable Ben Franklin was a lady killer in bed with the lasses. He was a lecherous, dirty old man and he said the best sex was with the older asses. He said that women age from the top down. First their faces and neck wrinkle, the tits sag and may deflate. The arms and belly get rolls of fat and the ass swells and hips widen. He observed that the only thing that never changes is the vagina. It is not necessary to throw a bag over an older women's head to use her. A dark room will suffice.

The older woman has been there, done that. She is very skilled to get the most satisfaction from a good fuck. He said most importantly, they are oh, so grateful.

BROADS CUSSING

As I have related in previous books, women are not always the cute, little harmless vixens they purport to be in polite company.

During WWII, I worked in a manufacturing plant with mostly older women whose husbands or boy friends were gone off to war.

These horny broads were constantly trying to lure me into a sexual alliance. They gossiped, dreamed and were voracious scavengers. I never heard so many dirty foul mouth talk any where else in my lifetime. Dirty jokes, boy could they tell them. It was "F" this and "F" everything all day long.

They act as if their ears are burning and oh, you are so crude to talk like that. Don't believe it, they are the real masters of shoveling shit.

Lookout for the coy, demure, standoffish barracudas, they will eat you alive and spit you out. After a fire and brimstone sermon in church, they have just sworn on a stack of bibles to change their wicked ways, but outside, in a millisecond they relent and want sex immediately. They are really hot to trot.

If you want confirmation of this to be true, just park outside a holy roller church and stop a beauty to hop in your car for some real fun-drinking and love making. Never fails - a sure thing.

Guess the female sex is just human after all. What could it hurt? If only again, wouldn't have had to spend so much bread in the past, if I had only practiced what I preached. Felt guilty being such a lecherous old man and hesitated to ask - insist - go for it. No problem you idiot! There for the taking. Try it, you'll like it. No remorse. If only.

Easy Pickings

I have noticed that the least pretty, rejected, neglected gals, make the best sure things for a score. They are anxious for attention and will satisfy you and tear you up in a nice, thankful way. Down, Roscoe. They'll use you, but what away to go. Just keep in the back of your mind as a panicky outlet. No big deal or fuss to get compliance. Oh, boy. Remember, they will be eager, willing and able to accommodate you at anytime in an emergency. Even after you are married. Mum's the word.

I am drawn to a woman's breasts. The teats have been shortened to tits. Boobs and jugs are other references to these appendages. Some are very attractive to look at. I like the period when young girls have pointed like little footballs projecting straight out of their chests. So cute and desirable to fondle. They are very inviting, especially if light pink to cherry red colored nipples. The really dark red ones not so pretty. If she is pregnant, I'm sure that whatever the shape or size her body produces milk to feed her baby.

The aureole, halo shaped, oval colored protuberance crowned by the nipple, can vary in size and shape, too. Some circles are huge, others medium, nice sized and some almost as small as on some men.

These two beauties are deliriously fun to fondle, kiss gently, lick and softly enclose the nipple in your teeth. This gets her attention and if they haven't become erect yet and she is aroused and ready for you to go south to the main attraction, the entrance to the Garden of Eden. Your rod should be satisfactorily erect and hard by now. You may enter the vagina and bang thrust away. Keep it in her and enjoy plowing away. Happy landing for you both.

MORE EUPHEMISMS

The names that men use to describe the vagina are not exactly terms of endearment. The cunt, the snatch, the twat, the box, etc., but the pussy is cute. It is a snapper alright.

After a few years of marriage, asking what she likes and prefers, the two of you can settle upon your favorite variations as far as different positions and a desirable tempo.

I know that as a young man at times I would, out of the blue, have a humongous erection and my balls, gonads, nuts, would feel as if they would explode if I didn't pound the shit out of it or have immediate sex. I would be obsessed with hauling my ashes and that was all that I could think of to satisfy those urges. I NEEDED SOME NOOKIE!

Usually during those young years, there was no easy, ready to lay babe around and I would have to pound the pud, jack off, pleasure myself to ease the misery. Self masturbation is common among both sexes and the women know how to get themselves to have an orgasm where quite often crude men fail miserably, women have electronic gadgets to vibrate them into ecstasy. Who needs a stud man?

Women have to check their breasts regularly to determine if there is an unusual lump and free of any. The ladies surely confide and gossip with others of the same sex. It's very important that they remind each other to do so. Cancer of the breast must be detected early. So important. Men always wonder, feel guilty, that maybe they were responsible by too rough handling of her tits.

One's mind plays perhaps the most important factor in activating the desire to have satisfying super sex. In our minds we think we can abuse these sensitive organs and over do it violently with too much exertion and usage. This can lead to over use and painful problems and needed cessation to calm down the tools and be able much later to engage again happily pain free.

I guess that's what makes a woman's breasts and vagina desirous is that it is forbidden fruit, rarely seen.

Other countries are exposed to them constantly and think "Ho hum, what's the big deal?"

Once again, the secrecy of our women works to their benefits as it makes the men wild to discover, touch and fondle. That grows old to some extent, soon enough.

There are so many ugly bodies out there that over exposure is a sure turn off. So what! Cover that crap up. Turn your head away. Think nothing's going on. I did not see that.

Men can visualize, hope they are right and guess at what is under the clothing of a babe. No assurance that in reality their dreams have any semblance to the truth and back to their imaginary perfect expectations. These are the best anyway.

A glimpse of stocking is somewhat shocking. Net stockings, lace panties and certain colors such as pink are a turn on for men. The sight and thought of what is hidden under is a sure turn on and in our caveman brains means "Mine, gotta have!" Whole lotta drooling going on.

The newspaper ads always feature pages of cute, untouchable panties and bras. Get out the old chastity box protective gear.

America rocks by getting their rocks off, have to break up your train of thought every once in a while.

Dangerous, Mean Little Women

The young girls today have tended to be very aggressive in their actions and demeanor. The more that they can emulate a man the better in their minds.

The little, no longer demure young ladies, but hell bent to be manlike - boylike. Today, the girls use dirty language cussing like drunken sailors.

They drive recklessly, at high speeds, and take their road rage out on any male driver on the road. It is as if, they throw caution to the wind and are apt to say that to hell with you, I'll show you that I'm better than any man. This has become a dangerous situation and exacerbated with them constantly blabbing on handheld phones.

I guess that as a man, I should feel sorry for them that they were not born as a male. If they only understood that most men envy them for all of the advantages which they have over a man.

Since the sexual freedom given them with the creation of the "pill" or device to ensure no pregnancy, they have become mad with power.

They demand to be an equal in all scenarios. They are never satisfied with their status nor station in life. They can no longer ever be trusted and a male must be on the caution to be stabbed in the back for a statement of his superiority at all times.

Money, power and greed has become their new identity. Anything goes, wearing no panties, flashing their crotches, revealing breasts - isn't this fun. No more rules and anything goes. Drugs, booze, sex with any and all anytime, anything goes - no danger in driving wildly drunk. So much more to be said. The times are changing and they have changed.

WOMEN WONDER ABOUT MEN, TOO

Perhaps more than you need to know reported by Harper's Magazine. "Women are more likely than men to ogle the genitals of a member of the opposite sex." "A study found, though in general people are more attracted to faces than to bodies." Men are assumed to not be manly were one to cry. From early childhood, a boy is taught that crying is out, not openly crying very often, men, seeing a woman cry, turn to putty, imploring the lass not to cry. Whatever is going on and what prompted the flow of tears, is put out of one's mind and attention is directed at soothing, calming the bawler.

Girls learn early on the power of melting down and crying to disarm and control the male sex.

During WWII, my mother, who never cried, locked herself in her bedroom and I could hear her sobbing for a long time. She was distraught, worried and helpless to do anything to find news of her many brothers and sisters and their children. They were in German occupied France and her letters were returned undeliverable.

The worst thing for her and for us, was not knowing if they were alive, whether any were ill and if they had enough to eat. My tears welled up!

We feared that "care" packages would be stolen and not get there to help them. We could have, should have, sent many more as after the war we learned how grateful they were to get one.

Men can't stand to witness a woman crying and it breaks our hearts. We relent and the little lady gets her way. Crying is a powerful weapon used by the weaker sex.

Maybe women exchange techniques while endlessly talking and refine their crying to have the ultimate advantage.

Having A Good Marriage

A good marriage takes effort on both of the parties involved. After all, the sexes of the two are different. Each grew up with different understandings of what makes a satisfactory and happy union. Thus, both have evolved in their hearts and their minds what they consider is the right way to go.

Therefore, one must listen carefully to each other and try to understand where the other is coming from. You must respect each other and love each other, overlooking differences and foreign to you of ways of thinking and doing things.

It ain't easy, camel's breath. It takes continuous patience and hard work. Paying strict attention to each other's needs and wants.

In a good situation, both parties know what the other is thinking and going to say. The two love birds become as one entity and even mimic one another and actually become to look like each other and act and react in unison, oblivious of the fact that it has become so.

You can anticipate quite accurately what the other is about to say or to do. You quickly get over the other's ideas and actions which you disagree with and they are soon swallowed and forgotten.

After all, you know each thing that the other one does which brings a pause, a frown, shake of your head, and a resolve to plow on, forgive and to accept. Just don't rub salt into any open wounds.

Okay, name five on your fingers, whom you admire and does all of these things?

There has to be a grain of truth in here somewhere.

PRO AND CON

For some of the following possible reasons and explanations of why some people stay together and some
   do not, a few guesses.
They really were compatible and love each other.
They are and were too lazy to seek other options.
They are too set in their ways to ever change.
Their religion bans and prohibits divorce.
They stay together for the sake of the kids.
They have no viable other choices.
They are waiting for the partner to die.
They don't have enough money to live alone.
One or the other is ill and needs help.
Nobody asked them to bug out and join them.
They actually enjoy bitching at one another.
They have no perceived notion of where to go.
They have no real good reason to leave.
They put up with each other for the good sex.
One controls all of the money.
They are too ugly to be wanted by others.
They never consider such a parting.
They might have to move out of their palace.
They worry of what friends might think.
They both would have to give up too much.
He beat her numerous times, but she stays.
He had a mistress or many.
She had her own outside lovers.
The grass is greener elsewhere.
One or both do not get enough attention.
They made a horrible mistake from the start.
He is impotent-she talks to much.
So you see that many reasons for staying together or to part are endless. Who knows why people do what
they do?

Humdrum Lives - Are Sports So Important

I was seated with a 92-year-old, former English lady at dinner and the subject came up about football. I asked her if she has seen, attended or watched football games. She answered, "Oh, yes. They run the ball, throw the ball and all fall down." I cracked up and all of the others at the table as well.

I have never heard such a short and simple explanation put so succinctly describing one of our revered national sporting games in my life. Right on and so true!

Face it, you have no control over a game's outcome. GROW UP!

Most people live vicariously through other perceived hero's. It is a matter of having decided to follow and to root for their favorite organization or sports team.

It all starts at a young age by being involved with a particular group or a team. Win or lose we are partial for our choice or involvement in the congregation club group and membership.

We become rabid fans and always feel if only I had a chance to be part of the action and to be revered, exalted and praised by others for my efforts and being a part of a winning team. By being at the game, we feel part of the big adventure.

We take our stance as having a favorite and will defend our choice forever no matter the cumulative record of our hero's. We get so carried away that in watching in the stands or on television that blood pressure rises to the danger point.

Since we live such humdrum lives, we go to great lengths to be part of the like-thinking hordes and must pay much money to get to an event and pay for parking, a program, the outrageous ticket prices for our seats and are further ripped off buying high priced food and drink.

In the final analysis, your attendance has little to do with the final. Outcome of the contest! Like lemmings, we follow the crowd and continue to try to be in on being proud of something beyond our control.

Women, more and more have joined in the something to do and can become more rabid fans.

Women follow, become involved with their team and gossip about games, too. As their men, they will defend their favorite by down in the dirt, hair pulling scraps with the woman who disagrees with them.

Athletics has become such an easy way to make big money, that the fun is lost in just playing the game. It is so humbling to back the losing team and now it has taken over our lives as we won't admit that we (their team stunk, screwed up, or were just plain out-played and deserved to lose.) Here comes the finger pointing and the excuses for failure. There is no self condemnation and always someone else or some other reason is the why they lost. Today, nobody will admit that it was an act of God and the fault lies elsewhere and others have to pay.

Our rabid indulgence in living through others has reached the point of being our way to create another universe to escape our own humdrum lives. Is this trip really necessary?

Since there is nothing which we can do about the outcome, why dwell on the impossible of our being center stage, adored and popular? Backing for the winner doesn't make us any smarter than the lowly, dejected losers.

Just wait till next year. We'll show you!

Ho, hum, humbug-humdrum. Is that all there is? You can read the sports page in the newspaper the next day and absorb the results much more easily and be proud of what you accomplished during that wasted time and money wasted in such humdrum goings on.

I have pride and I have my favorite teams and am happy for them for the winning side, but I do not frame my life on whether they have won or lost.

DID SHE TELL?

Over use of everything can lead to unneeded consequences. Everything in moderation is the best policy. Too much, too often can lead to a complete shut down and flood of excuses why not to do it.

Are these private moments, number of times performed and their feelings widely discussed and included in a gal's gossiping? Makes a man to wonder what her girl friend is thinking when facing him. Guilty or not, he feels caught and exposed. Whether true or not.

A man never can know what goes on and is talked about in hen sessions among women. Maybe they all know that you couldn't get it up and how often and how many times? What a horrible thing to have to worry about. Damned gossiping.

Women all of their lives are so secretive that men fear the worst that the whole world knows that he couldn't perform because he couldn't get it up. Men fuss, worry and wonder never knowing if exposed for sure.

Women will be women, God love them, but they keep and retain secrets so well and control their man by cutting him off from sexual exploits at any time and for any reason. The hapless clod is helpless in this woman's world.

Gals out live their little boy playthings and live to inherit all accumulated wealth over their union. The world is their oyster and cannot be cracked nor defeated.

We must pity the poor male slob who goes through life always wondering what the ladies say and gossip about. Could lead to drink and a neurosis to not trust anybody.

I am going to have to go to bed until all of this gossip and sexual revelations passes. I am drained and have to shut up! You are exhausted too, but thanks for coming along for the ride.

ANON

Little lie there!

AHEAD, REAL DANGER-WORRIES

The 2008 election could be the end of our system of life and our economy. The threat of a democrat gaining the presidency of the United States is very frightening. Both houses in jeopardy, too!

The democrat aspirants are liberal, lovers of big government and active proponents for socialism and government bureaucracy in control of all of our lives forever. Care for us from the womb to the tomb.

They feel and believe that they, and only they, should know what is best for everybody. Of course with the unions, African Americans, Hollywood and newly burgeoning Hispanic-Latinos, Jews, Catholics, who always vote for handouts of your money, will soon outnumber sane, thinking conservatives and run this country into the ground. Socialism has failed worldwide.

Like 20 plus years ago when the Chicago Tribune, noted in my book titled "What We Have Here and Why", showed that our government bureaucracy already had grown back then to be the biggest landowner, property manager, renter, mover and hauler, medical clinician, lender, insurer, mortgage broker, employer, debtor, taxer and spender in all history and it has grown worse since and those running for office have much more plans to add to this atrocity and ensure their control and reelection forever. Third world country, here we come.

They Outnumber The Sane

These scoundrels, since "Social Security," have incrementally created more and more programs to give handouts to groups of people, who, instead of taking responsibility for their own lives, now demand and expect the tooth fairy, Uncle Sam, to dole out other's hard earned taxes to save these indigents and unworthy blood suckers and insure their existence and locked in votes forever. Worldwide, socialism has failed miserably.

Once created, these programs are never dissolved and continue to expand assuring continuous votes for the socialists. These high paid administrators of this largesse have lifetime positions of shame on your money.

Socialism is a cancer that grows and never can be stopped. We have and had no choice but to pay the government to use these newly acquired funds to blow it on more schemes, to use the monies to acquire more votes by dribbling little drabs here and there and they know it, but are happy as hell with their insistence that we're all stupid and need their help forever. After all, it is their money and not yours. RIGHT?

The sky is falling.

THE DOMINO THEORY

Some pundits propose that we open the borders to the illegal immigrants. They will buy houses on mortgage and pay their interest and their taxes not having decent jobs, no earnings? OH!

This would be the first tile to knock down and the next add nausea. The social security system, Medicare and health expenses will balloon like topsy. The additional pressure on big, socialist, big daddy would become enormous.

The liberal socialists will raise taxes to try to cover and reduce these atrocities and it will never be enough. Hence, our booming economy will come to a screeching slow down and halt. A nice depression for us all and a chance for our loving, big bureaucracy, socialistic, fairy god mother will be there to salve the bleeding hearts. Our saviors!

These scoundrels who are the elite democrats will love it and ensure their automatic hold to control of the bloated government forever. More votes for the democrats.

The end for this great country, our worldwide admiration and crash to becoming a third world status.

The dominos are in place to tumble in sequence and can't be stopped once set in motion. A huge increase in suicides and they will be the lucky ones. Adios, aurevoir, auf wiedersehn. Whatever you call it. Loo out!

Worth gossiping about. IF ONLY!

Political Correctness Gone Awry And To The Absurd

Guy, chap, fellow, man's name, leader by definition. Somehow, the women have wedged their way into being recognized as one of the guys.

They are delirious over being included in this special long accepted meaning of the word. They have come to work it into almost every conversation.

I suspect that they are so happy with this turn of events that they may even wet their panties at having in their minds arrived at equal status with their male counterparts.

This is just one of the intentional, idiotic, political injections into everyday vocabulary, which is demeaning and creating havoc in our society. Right guys?

This sort of inclusion is one of the many reasons that women have changed too - "I'm your equal" sort of reasoning and to increased aggressiveness. It has to be stopped before it is too late and divides forever the sexes.

Don't get me started on the poison of political correctness. It has become so wide spread that perfectly good words and their true meaning can no longer be used in ordinary conversation. One has to carefully consider any potential misunderstanding by others first before saying anything.

One can be frowned upon for not adhering to the new rules of speech. Horse feathers, madness, idiocy, useless, painful, ridiculous and a bunch of crap. Eat these road apples. Apox on them! Say what you mean to say and don't worry or make any excuses or wonder if you did right? These strict constructionists are just silly liberals. They want everything to be run by a socialist federal government from the cradle to the grave.

In this litigious society, loo out! If one has lots of money and it is widely known, it can be a curse.

For any and all reasons, one can be sued for outrageous amounts of money and your life can come to a standstill.

The greedy attorneys know that their fees can mean easy street for them and they will go after their quarry like junkyard dogs.

Once a person is accused of anything, from that moment on, you are assumed guilty. Even if found not guilty, the perception-memory of the accusation lingers forever. Your life is ruined, shame on you, don't meet them face-to-face, cross the street to avoid this horrible person.

In this age, one can be sued for outrageous amounts of money and the liberal judges and courts allow huge settlements over nothing. You can never again be trusted, be seen in public, and the redistribution of wealth leaches are in their element of hysteria and glee.

After the lynching is over, there is no way to recover one's past good name.

The liberal judges have taken it upon themselves to create new laws and ignore the only true law making bodies designated in our constitution.

Sue, the old system of it was an act of God, not your fault, and "Sorry you were so stupid to have failed to take care of yourself", and somebody else is responsible, "not me," is the norm.

The eternal gripe is that others have more money than you do. The socialists feel that it is not right and something has to be done about it. We must redistribute the wealth and the demos mean it. Tax more the wealthy people and companies. They do not deserve to have more and must have stolen it from the poor people.

The students today are taught and made to believe that all companies should not be allowed to make a profit.

The incentive to better oneself and move up into a higher income bracket is being stymied. That money that you have slaved for is not yours. The socialistic bureaucracy big government must be in charge of your life and wealth.

Greed and power is the way of life and desired liberal way of doing things. They point at rich republicans and it is they who are the wealthiest and being in charge and on top of running things are smug in their control of everything as everybody else is too stupid to care for themselves.

Smile, lie, cheat, pontificate, tell the big lie often enough and they will believe us and we will retain our power and control over those idiots. Give the poor, the ignorant and lowly creatures a little bit of money now and then and they will love us and vote for us forever. These are trying times.

Wake up America, throw the bastards out of power! Don't let the wackos take over this great country!

God help us if one Hillary Clinton wins nomination to be the next president of the United States of America and wins.

Not only does she want to raise your taxes, but she is a confirmed socialist. We would have the first woman to hold this coveted position of power, but she would appear to be more like a man as she always wears long pants to cover her wide hips.

The broad, how can she continue to dress this way is a mystery. Surely she will have to be wearing a nice dress for meeting visiting dignitaries and no form fitting evening dresses at formal affairs. What a horrible thought and disaster.

Has anyone asked her why she only had one child? She must have been too much in love with gaining power and being aggressive to get ahead to be bothered with more motherhood.

She has blocked all release of her personal diaries or important papers of her participation and activities in her husband's presidency. We know many of her shenanigans.

If this information of her background were available to the responsible voting public, it would be all over for her and for once she couldn't lie her way out of the truth.

Get down on your knees and pray that she not win and succeed in her strong-armed take over of this country and impose a socialist regime here. Is that really her hair? Danger is lurking in this scenario for us all!

OBSERVATIONS

We are now engaged in an exaggerated, doom's day hysteria over the new scare tactic, called global warming. Madness-gore-stupid Nobel Peace prize.

The truth, the facts, the common sense investigation of these allegations and claims are proof that this is an idiotic exercise.

Record keeping reports that the hottest year in history, was 1934. If you were alive back then, you would know that 1935 and 1936-7-8 etc, were extremely hot too. Many other times, too.

Our weather patterns run in cycles and we may expect blistering cold winters to come in the future. All very normal. The sky is not falling.

The American resolve to defeat terrorists and terrorism is undermined by the bleeding heart liberals who want us to withdraw our troops from Afghanistan and Iraq.

We never lost any major engagement in the war in Vietnam, but the same cry babies demonstrated and eventually forced our withdrawal and not true, our defeat.

Pulling out from there only emboldens our enemies who again would say that "See there, they are paper tigers." We have never lost a war when backed by the American people and we shouldn't make that mistake again.

The lunatic, tree hugging, radicals are denying us from drilling for new oil wells. Nimby, not in my backyard for oil cracking refineries to produce more gasoline. No to safe atomic energy. 150 years of coal reserves. More trees in this country in all history.

FOR GOD'S SAKE

Free enterprise and capitalism is the only answer, not socialism.

Before it's too late, wake up America. Most of us are so busy with our own lives that we do not see nor realize what is happening to us and what is going on. Rape the little folks.

The left wing, radical, wacko, liberal, socialists are in no hurry to incrementally erode common sense and continue to increase bureaucracy and big government. It has been working already too long.

It has worked for the democrats and recently conservatives have fallen under their dangerous spell and we are just now vetoing their absolutely wrong attempts to push through legislation which will rapidly escalate the costs of their so-called nice give-aways to buy votes.

Take back control of this country before it is too late. Think what these horrible new ideas and bills will do to us and mean to everyone in the future.

Private enterprise through competition results in much lower costs for us to pay. The government is not business men wise and anything which they take control of results in a disastrous situation which we can't get out of and escalates with out stopping forever.

LORD HELP US!

Do nothing and suffer the loss of everything which made us stand out and enjoy in the past.

VOTE REPUBLICAN!

A WOMAN PRESIDENT

I have nothing against having a female to lead this great country. But, I emphatically am against such an error at this point in time.

We are at war and spread too thin. Today, the old situation of two countries facing off against one another, face-to-face and hand-to-hand, is not the scenario today.

The use of air power, tanks, rockets and infantry is not applicable right now. Wars bog down to where we have to fight groups of terrorists supplied by other anti-American countries and it is hard to show land taken and verifiable advancements and victories.

Our people liken this war to our war in Vietnam. Not so, camel's breath. The Vietcong were supplied by China and Russia and it was a war against a country and not pockets of insurgents.

Now we have Russia supplying Iran who wants to take over Iraq and control all of the oil capacities of that complete region. The whole world would be in danger if they were to get atomic bombs and the loss of the oil from there would be disastrous and very crippling.

Russia is as bad as France in trying to reclaim former world respect and power. They are poised to control all of Europe by use of their huge oil reserves and keeping it from the Euros. China is building an immense military of troops, tanks, rockets, airpower and navy. These are trying and dangerous times.

I personally feel that a man is better to resolve and handle these great problems. Men who have been in war, and know that it is hell, are better equipped emotionally to serve in these perilous times.

There are more women voters in this country and I can understand their excitement to look forward to at last, have a woman as president. Many other countries have had women in control of their homelands and have done good jobs there, but not in what is, let's face it, a world to control and dangerous.

I realize that as women, mothers and love and worry about their husbands and male children, do not like, nor want any fighting, nor wars. At times, it is necessary to protect our way of life and our country and to fight for our survival. Never a pretty picture, but has to be done. Can she do that?

We can't have a leader who vacillates, waits too long to get involved and in the end could wind up losing by deciding to wait too long.

Not that women can't be strong, but they tend to mess around and hope to talk their way out of trouble and seldom working and could put our backs to the wall.

Although it may be a nice change of power, exciting and fun for the ladies to have achieved their goal to be completely and even better than men, we just plain, flat out, can't take the chance of playing what if?

On top of all of these important reasons, why not to have a woman president now even more devastating for us would be the present front runner woman may create a completely socialistic country, raise taxes and take us downhill to perdition.

I hope and pray that our ladies will have the good sense while gossiping to consider what common sense that I have pointed out and use their amazing intuition and superior brains to agree that unfortunately it is just not the time to back and install a very questionable woman to be president at this time. No doubt in the near future a great woman will be chosen to run this country by acclamation by both of the major parties.

I thank you in advance for being so smart and rejecting this unsavory woman to trick you into voting for her. You may have just saved this country. That woman's past is so bad that she just cannot be trusted.

For me, for asking the question, what do women gossip about, I feel that I have a little better understanding now.

Women, jolly well have a lot to talk about and a real need to be secretive about many things.

The government, the military services, and women, it all boils down to the need to know. Fair enough.

STORYTIME

He rambled, he rambled, he rambled all around, in and out of town, until he finally settled down. He and his wife stayed where he had found a home.

One day he came face to face with a mean bitch who didn't like his being in town. They argued and knowing that it was fruitless to converse with the bimbo, he turned away from her and started to walk away.

She pulled out a gun and shot him in the back, killing him. His killer was let go as she lied and claimed self defense.

His wife would not let that decision stand and rambled door-to-door to find this maniac. She rambled through the swinging doors to a rowdy bar and asked had anyone seen this murderer? "Just left," she was told and headed south. Off rambled the wife after the culprit, her pistol gleaming in the noon day sun.

Upon meeting up with the woman and confronting her. The hooker pulled out her gun. The loving wife rambled away having shot the killer down.

The moral of this story is that a wife, woman will stand up for, protect, and standby, defend her man to the end.

WE BOYS-MEN FIGHT BACK, TOO

During the 1930's depression, we, boys all had bikes. We quite often met at Zent's garage as outdoors was a device which one could set to read how much air one had used to inflate your tires.

Back in that era, many people rode bikes great distances and would come through our town on their journey. One day, while getting air in our tires, an older kid from out of town pulled up to talk to us kids.

He made the mistake of calling our gang "small town rubes." Ted, a left hander, took offense at those fighting words. Both he and the interloper put up their dukes.

If you have ever fought a left handed boxer, you know that the left is their most powerful arm and a punch comes at you in a blur from that unexpected side.

Ted gave him a haymaker shot square on his chin and down he went on his ass. He pedaled a hasty retreat out of town.

The girls saw this atrocity by we mean boys and were gossiping about the crude boys. Moral of the story.

You see, we, boys-men defend our turf, our country and our women folk.

POET AUGUSTUS JOHN. I SKETCHED HIM OFF OF TELEVISION

SUMMARY AND SUNSET

Perhaps all of that lifetime of harboring secrets is why so many more women are in church asking forgiveness for their sins. The fairer sex feels guilty for all of the times that they gave in too easily to achieve some perceived want or goal. They regret having done so many spur of the moment no nos.

The men in their lives have never completely gotten over their suspicions of what their mates are up to nor what they might have done.

Fortunately for all men, the women have spent all of their lives nurturing and caring and are even more understanding and attentive to them in both of their old ages.

OK, we males will never know what women gossip about and the mystery can never be solved. Oh, maybe they are talking about . . .? Wrong, give up and get on with it! We men have a tendency to keep everything inside of us - think, surmise the worst and better confess our sins of commission and omission, too.

Let's put these observations to rest and as is our ordained pleasure of looking out for and loving our ladies, get on with our lives.

Sunset, behind the western hills, the weary sun goes down. Another day has taken flight, our day, our task is done. The cool of night comes on. Here let me drop my pen and wait tomorrow's dawn.

THE LAST WORD

It is done.
This is the end.
Maybe I could have made it better.
The book is done.
I offer you this,
It may not be exactly what I dreamed of.
It's not all that I planned it to be.
I have labored with inexperience,
And dreamed in terms that I knew little of.
This is the end.
My task is done.
Deal kindly with me,
Knowing that I tried.

As Lawrence Welk Always Said, "Keep A Song In Your Heart"

You must remember this,
A kiss is still a kiss,
A sigh is just a sigh.
The fundamental things in love,
* As time goes by.
And when two lovers woo,
They still say I love you,
On that you can rely
The world will always
Welcome lovers,
* As time goes by.
* Song title of PBS TV show.
Remember to bonk someone today, or is it boink? Whichever, do it, you'll both feel better.
If you don't use it, you lose it.
At 80 years old, be prepared as it is pretty much down hill from there on.

I recommend that all of you contact my publisher Author House and order all three of my other books.

The first one is titled, "Noodling and Canoodling Around." Be sure to look up the main meanings of canoodling. In the old days, it was in use in conversation quite often.

The second book is titled, "I'm Glad You Got To See Me!" As with all of my books, there is some semblance of humor in them. This book has pictures of some of my artistic endeavors. You'll enjoy it.

The third book is titled, "What We Have Here and Why." It contains my take on how this country has been incrementally eroded, some surprising past indignities foisted upon us by the French. The crowning achievement is excerpts from Barry Goldwater's book, "The Conscience of a Conservative."

All four of my books have a picture on the cover of some of my artwork. Try them, you'll like them.

For God commands the angels to guard you in all your ways (Psalm 91:11). See you on the other side!

Norman Andre Richards

Printed in the United States
118202LV00002B